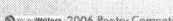

"I have a dream that my four little children will one day live in a nation where they will not be judged by the color of their skin, but by the content of their character."

Martin Luther King

I have a dream
words to change the world

- MOTIVATE your pupils to write and appreciate poetry.
- INSPIRE them to share their hopes and dreams for the future.
- BOOST awareness of your school's creative ability.
- WORK alongside the National Curriculum or the high level National Qualification Skills.
- Supports the *Every Child Matters* - Make a Positive Contribution outcome.
- Over £7,000 of great prizes for schools and pupils.

"When I was out there I was never ever alone, there was always a team of people behind me, in mind if not in body."
Ellen MacArthur

Eastern Counties Vol II
Edited by Carrie Ghazanfer

First published in Great Britain in 2006 by:
Young Writers
Remus House
Coltsfoot Drive
Peterborough
PE2 9JX
Telephone: 01733 890066
Website: www.youngwriters.co.uk

All Rights Reserved

© Copyright Contributors 2006

SB ISBN 1 84602 525 7

Foreword

Imagine a teenager's brain; a fertile yet fragile expanse teeming with ideas, aspirations, questions and emotions. Imagine a classroom full of racing minds, scratching pens writing an endless stream of ideas and thoughts . . .

. . . Imagine your words in print reaching a wider audience. Imagine that maybe, just maybe, your words can make a difference. Strike a chord. Touch a life. Change the world. Imagine no more . . .

'I Have a Dream' is a series of poetry collections written by 11 to 18-year-olds from schools and colleges across the UK and overseas. Pupils were invited to send us their poems using the theme 'I Have a Dream'. Selected entries range from dreams they've experienced to childhood fantasies of stardom and wealth, through inspirational poems of their dreams for a better future and of people who have influenced and inspired their lives.

The series is a snapshot of who and what inspires, influences and enthuses young adults of today. It shows an insight into their hopes, dreams and aspirations of the future and displays how their dreams are an escape from the pressures of today's modern life. Young Writers are proud to present this anthology, which is truly inspired and sure to be an inspiration to all who read it.

Contents

Norwich High School for Girls, Norwich

Alex Morris (11)	1
Rachel Moxon (13)	2
Kathryn Lines (14)	3
Gemma Lam (14)	4
Freya Hocking (13)	5
Naveen Rizvi (13)	6
Chloe France (13)	7
Emily Wesby (11)	8
Hannah Rhodes (14)	9
Sophia Thompson (14)	10
Natalie Bayton (12)	11
Marie Mallinder (14)	12
Alice Whitehead (11)	12
Jane Shaker (11)	13
Rosie Cooke (11)	13
Olivia Martin (11)	14
Camilla Le Coq (12)	15
Kelly Hunter (12)	16
Hetty Stephen (12)	16
Pippa Jones (11)	17
Lucy Temple (12)	18
Milly Larner (11)	19
Rachael Hopley (11)	20
Jessica Beattie (12)	20
Hatty Ekbery (11)	21
Tamzin Steggles (11)	21
Elizabeth Bamber (11)	22
Aimi Eagle (11)	23
Laura Butters (12)	24
Georgina Rhead (12)	24
Sammy Haycox (11)	25
Madi Brown (12)	25
Victoria Proctor (11)	26
Katie Ackers (12)	26
Mary Wheeler (11)	27
Helen Baxter (11)	27
Alice Rickett (12)	28
Eleanor Stanley (12)	28

Mary Peart (13)   29
Charlotte Randle (11)   29
Katherine Furniss (13)   30
Millie Farrant (12)   31
Rebecca Wooldridge (11)   32
Brontë Goodwin (11)   33
Sasha Baynham (11)   33
Ellen Kirby (13)   34
Rachel Mumford (13)   35
Rosie Vavasour (12)   36
Jess Collinson (12)   37
Lucy Hardy (13)   38
Sara-Jayne Williams (13)   39

Reepham High School, Norwich
Luke Sewell (12)   39
Liam Waller (12)   40
Carla Woodcock (11)   40
Helen Betts (12)   41
Eryn Kirkcaldy (11)   41
Oliver Rayner (12)   42
Jack Wardle (12)   42
Vicki Giles (12)   42
Jake Pearce (11)   43
Bradley Graves (11)   43
Rosie Feltham (12)   43
Christopher Forrest (11)   44
Megan Watling (12)   44
Deanna Cooper (12)   44
Sarah Roberts (12)   45
Louise Bugg (12)   45
Chloe Dunton (11)   46
Henry Skinner (11)   46
Sophie Speer (12)   47
Nick Davis (11)   47
Polly Randell-Bateman (12)   48
Becky Manton (12)   49
Michaela Crane (11)   49
Jordan McDowall (12)   50
Emma Osborne (11)   50
Sophie Maddox (11)   51

Maddy Vogler (12)	51
Emma Godwin (13)	52
Tasha Ferenczy (12)	53
Samuel Whittaker (11)	54
Leon Allen (13)	54
Natasha Wade (11)	55
Alice Searjeant (12)	55
Tayla Menear (12)	56
Amy Secker (12)	56
Charlie Skinner (11)	57
Steven Parker (11)	57
Catrin Hamer (12)	58
Toni Hall (13)	58
Sián Sands (12)	59
Grant Cattermull (11)	59
Megan Cross-Gower (13)	60
Frankie Fuller (11)	61
Shelley Cook (11)	61
Emma Skidmore (12)	61
Joshua Kennedy (12)	62
Jacob Mears (12)	62
Lily Tozer (12)	63
Dean Francis (13)	63
Cameron Clapton (12)	64

Riverside Middle School, Bury St Edmunds

Anna Brown (13)	65
Ellie Clarke (11)	66
Karla Abrey (11)	67
Ashley Hegan (11)	68
Natalie Beckwith (12)	68
Charmaine Harris-Harvey (12)	69
Sally Fung (12)	69
Tom Gillingham (12)	70
Ryan White (12)	71
Ryan Nutter (11)	72
Danielle Taylor (11)	73
Millie Royal (12)	74
Emily Carter (12)	75

St Andrew's School, Bedford

Katelina Fusco (14)	76
Victoria Elms (13)	76
Sarah Eve (14)	77
Louise Brentnall (15)	77
Eleanor Roblett (12)	78
Laura Batchelor (11)	79
Kimberley Ambrose (11) & Charlotte Northwood (12)	80
Kelly Alston (15)	81
Hannah Lewis & Zoe Blair (11)	82
Verity Esaw (13)	83
Claire Bushell (14)	84
Caroline Watson (11)	84
Deanna Winn (12)	85
Emma Hind (12)	85
Sejal Chandarana (12)	86
Emily Hillier (12)	87
Sophie Richardson (13)	88
Gabriella Farrow (12)	89
Nicola Brentnall (13)	90
Charlotte Walker (12)	90
Lucy Darnell (14)	91
Fraya Brinkman (11)	91
Holly Wheldon	92
Rebecca Brinkley (13)	93
Holly Holt (13)	94
Caroline Watson (12)	95
Amandeep Rai (12)	95
Carrie-Ann Minty (13)	96

Sandye Place School, Sandy

Katie Garner (13)	96
Chris Gregory (13)	97
Jack Tortoise (12)	98
Adam McGrath (12)	99
Sharnie Partridge (12)	100
Jordan Leigh (13)	101
Carla Dring (12)	102
Joseph Olaniran (12)	103
Tom Hull (11)	104

Carly Brinkley (12)	105
Josie Bullock (11)	106
Laura Jones (12)	107
Andrew Robinson (11)	108
Lawrence Franklin (13)	109
Naomi Morris (12)	110
Arron Davies-Sond (12)	111
Brian Andrew (13)	112
Sabina Nessa (13)	113
Lisa Stevens (13)	114
Donna West (11)	114
Ashley Rees (12)	115
Shaun Chapman (12)	115
Lola Idris (12)	116
George Hutson (12)	117
Kelly Wall (12)	118
Daniel Olaniran	118
Hanna Chupryna (12)	119
Shane Poulter	119
Frances Bell (12)	120
Thomas Hunt (12)	121
Joe Keir (12)	122
Daniel Day (12)	123
Imogen Partridge (11)	124
Michael Bodi (12)	124
Arron McLoughlin (12)	125
Lauren Keeble (12)	125
Danielle Hutchinson (11)	126
Emma Jeffery (11)	127
Rioni Williams (11)	128
Jessica Brown (11)	128
Camellia Fage (11)	129
Kelly Evans (11)	129
Nigel Adams (12)	130
Lucy Barringer (13)	131
Natalie Broughall (13)	132
Jake Cooper (12)	133
Jack Parish (11)	134
Robert Tant (12)	135
Scott Parsons (13)	135

Jordan Harrington (11)	136
Brett Slater (13)	137
Danielle Coveney (13)	138
Jasmine Phillips (12)	139
Rosemary Robertson (12)	139

Sawston Village College, Sawston

Pippa Bransfield-Garth (13)	140
Kirstie Bransfield-Garth (12)	141
Emily Driscoll (12)	142
Tom Bell (13)	142
Ben Miller (13)	143
Zuhair Crossley (11)	143
Alix Schwiening (13)	144
David Ford (12)	145
Spinoza Pitman (13)	146
Tom Champness (15)	147
Sam Fleck (13)	148
Rhys James (13)	149
Alex Scally (14)	150

Sawtry Community College, Sawtry

Sophie Banks (12)	150
Emma Ladlow (12)	151
Anelise Rosa (13)	152
Michael Gutsell (12)	153
Megan Curtis (13)	154
Chelsea Owen (13)	154
Jordan Marsh (11)	155
Hannah Smith (12)	156
Jordan Cooke (13)	156
Penelope Ford (12)	157
Jessica Halley (11)	157
Emily Wilson (11)	158
Ben Reed (13)	158
Fern Cornwall	159

Sunnyside School (SLD), Biggleswade
    Leon Stenhouse (17)   159
    Rory Simpson (14)   160
    Rosie Chappell (17)   160

Swavesy Village College, Swavesy
    James Barker (14)   161

The Poems

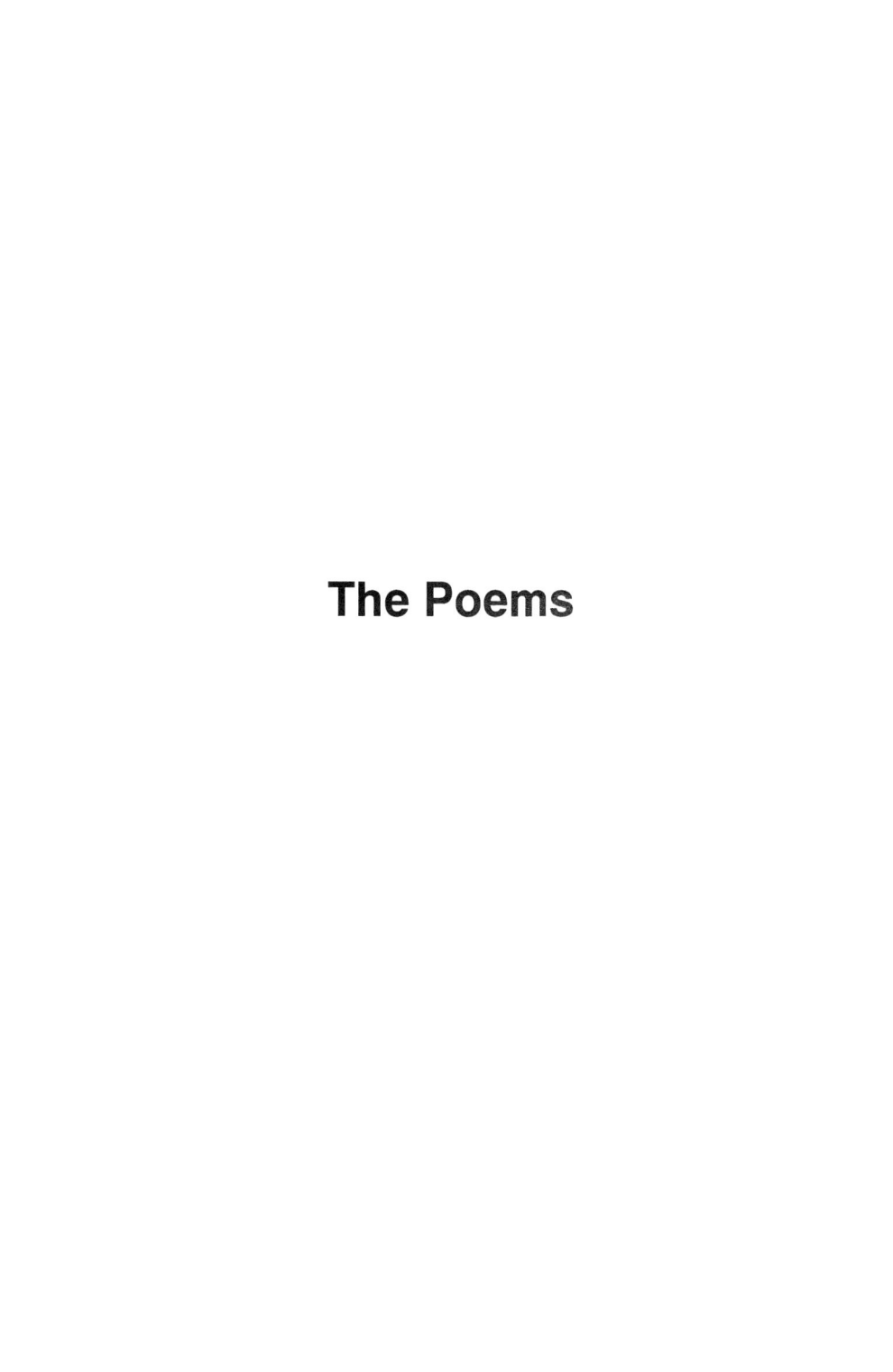

I Have A Dream

I have a dream
That cruelty is stopped,
It just isn't fair,
I wish it were dropped.

Cruelty to the kids
And animals too,
Just neglecting them,
We should them sue.

If violence stopped,
The world would be a happier place,
It would be great,
If we didn't have limited space.

We should respect,
Children and other creatures well
As they have rights
And they have special features.

We should give love,
To our sisters and brothers
And always think
Of all the others.

Then out of the blue,
Violence would go,
It would stop there,
So blood or flesh would not show.

I never guessed life would be so harsh,
Then keep it locked away,
Maybe in a prison cell,
I hope this will happen one day.

Alex Morris (11)
Norwich High School for Girls, Norwich

My Dream

This is my dream,
My vision of the future,
Unique to me,
But with the same ideals
As the person sitting next to me.

I dream that the world is free
No global warming or political barriers.
As free as the clouds, skidding on the breeze;
As free as the waves, tossing their stormy manes.

We have stopped trying to extend limits
That should never have been bent.
Death is now accepted, not shunned.
Crime is non-existent.
Doors are not locked.

Equality is now commonplace, without extremes.
Hatred is gone, banished forever.
Children of all races, creeds, colours, nationalities,
Play together in sunny pastures.

Nature has reclaimed her crown,
She has righted the balance.
We have all stopped competing
For the *ultimate supremacy;*
We all know it doesn't matter.

Pollution is no more
The planet is respected.
War has fled, never to return,
She was banished with her mother, Hatred.

Peace and unity reign once more,
With Joy and a tinge of Sorrow.
Poverty has been broken,
Cracked open like a brittle nutshell,
To reveal a hollow centre.

This is my dream,
My vision of the future,
Unique to me,
But with the same ideals
As the person sitting next to me.

Rachel Moxon (13)
Norwich High School for Girls, Norwich

I Have A Dream

Equality, democracy,
Freedom to speak aloud,
United, bonded, together as one,
Standing tall, free and proud.

No hatred, scorn or criminal acts,
No fighting, anger or war,
No racism, communism, sexism or ageism,
No depression behind a closed door.

I have a dream,
A dream of a better future,
A future for the next generation,
The generation we thought we were.

No climate change or meltdowns,
No more rising of the seas,
No more whales lost up the Thames,
No lost honey from the bees.

Bonjour, joll sun, hallo,
Aslamlaecom, hello,
Communications between our country neighbours,
Unlike our fearsome wartime ancestors.

I have a dream,
A dream in a fantasy place,
In reality, it is but a dream,
In endless time and space.

Kathryn Lines (14)
Norwich High School for Girls, Norwich

I Have A Dream

When I was young, I never had a dream,
Except the ones of joy, of fun, of happiness,
But now I'm older, and the world vision I had
Disappeared,
I see pain, suffering and sadness,
I have a dream, a dream to see through those eyes,
That I once had.

Our loved ones protect us from the sad
And offer us the good,
There are many goods, but just as many bad,
But the world is not as simple as good
And bad.
When we are bad we find that we are alone,
When we are good we find that we are free,
I have a dream, a dream that everyone in the world is free.

God made us as equals,
Whether we are fat or thin, clever or dumb,
A millionaire living in a mansion, or a beggar living on the streets.
How we look doesn't define who we are,
It's what we do that does,
Why do models get recognised, while scientists don't?
I have a dream, a dream that people are equal,
Just the way God made us.

There are some people who give,
They give their hearts, their trust and their time,
But sometimes we need a helping hand from someone who
Is willing to give,
Without getting anything back,
Why do we ignore the help we get
And never appreciate what we receive?
I have a dream, a dream that every person who gives,
Will get something back in return.

Gemma Lam (14)
Norwich High School for Girls, Norwich

I Had A Dream

The lights flickered,
He had a dream,
The children still cried and whimpered,
He had a dream.

Women hurried through the streets as dusk,
He had a dream,
People with guns killed the innocent,
He had a dream.

And so did I,
I dreamt of equality, democracy, white weddings and joy,
No hunger, misery or want,
Ever entered my idealist visions.

But still, after so long,
The little children walk for miles for water,
Their heads stooping, blisters gnawing their feet,
Distorted by life.

He had a dream, like mine,
Of peace and contentment,
No war and strife,
Life, like *one big birthday party*.

But wait, isn't life like a birthday party?
The focus on a few people, rich with presents,
Some not invited, and some too greedy,
Then the clowns, with painted faces, hiding their feelings.

He had a dream,
I had a dream,
But those dreams are no more,
Shattered by reality.

We had a dream,
They had a dream,
But they have become memories and myths,
We still have dreams, but they are fading.

Freya Hocking (13)
Norwich High School for Girls, Norwich

I Have A Dream . . .

I have a dream . . .
To play for a football team,
To become supreme,
To swim an ocean,
To see the world in slow motion,
To sing in an opera,
Especially an aria,
To climb a mountain,
To visit the Trevi Fountain,
To see the world,
To see my life unfold,
To walk to the North Pole,
To follow my soul,
To find the cure for cancer,
To meet the Pink Panther,
To run in the London marathon,
To become a nun.
To travel abroad,
To meet the one and only Lord,
To see my grandchildren live,
To ride the locomotive,
To meet Santa Claus,
To dedicate myself to a cause,
To give blood,
To hold a lotus bud,
To play with my band,
To make a stand,
To see different races rejoice,
To see everyone make the right choice,
To see a child say 'No' to drugs,
To see a kangaroo give its baby a hug,
To walk on the moon,
To witness a butterfly escape from its cocoon,
To see the world at peace,
To live in a world drawn by Matisse.

I have a dream . . .
About all my wishes coming true.

Naveen Rizvi (13)
Norwich High School for Girls, Norwich

The End Of . . .

I have a dream,
No struggling, sorrow, endless yearning,
Wise, happy people, learning,
Worry, stress, a thing of the past,
Anxiety, needs to be gone at last,
No longer feeding the family, sore, blistered feet,
In a cool classroom, out of the heat,
No disease, they're too wise now,
To AIDS do they no longer have to bow,
I have a dream, the end of poverty.

I have a dream,
We value our privileges, they satisfy our need,
The bountiful sea of greed recedes,
Gratitude is a commonplace,
No moans, or grudges, not a whining face,
Instead of cars, mansions, villas,
Our money is fed to the most notorious killers,
We think about what we buy,
Fair trade is no longer a myth or lie,
I have a dream, the northern hemisphere
Have aided the stricken south out of despair.

I have a dream,
No struggling, sorrow, endless yearning,
We value our privileges, they satisfy our need,
Worry, stress, a thing of the past,
Our money is fed to the notorious killers,
No longer feeding the family, blistered feet,
The news isn't full of famine and disease,
Africa, no longer ruled by selfish leaders,
Trade, famine, water shortage aren't on the agenda,
I have a dream that the Third World no longer exists.

Chloe France (13)
Norwich High School for Girls, Norwich

I Wish For A World Of Peace, Paradise, Utopia

I wish for a world with no war or harm,
I wish for a world of peace,
I wish for a world which is quiet and gentle,
Peace, paradise, Utopia.

I wish for a world with no global warming,
I wish for a world unspoilt,
I wish for a world which is peaceful and safe,
Peace, paradise, Utopia.

I wish for a world where there is no hunting,
I wish for a world of animals,
I wish for a world where the dodo still roams,
Peace, paradise, Utopia.

I wish for a world where there are no cars,
I wish for a world of walking,
I wish for a small world where people could walk,
Peace, paradise, Utopia.

I wish for a world with no hunger or thirst,
I wish for a world of equality,
I wish for a world which has endless supplies,
Peace, paradise, Utopia.

I wish for a world with no crimes or criminals,
I wish for a world of love,
I wish for a world where everyone is happy,
Peace, paradise, Utopia.

I wish for a world where this may be true,
I wish for a world of dreams,
I wish for a world which is perfect and friendly,
My peace, my paradise, my Utopia.

Emily Wesby (11)
Norwich High School for Girls, Norwich

I Have A Dream

I have a dream,
A vision of the future,
That all around the world,
There will be no torture.

I have a vision,
A wonderful fantasy,
Of all the people,
Praising God for eternity.

I have an idea,
Everyone dancing,
All day, all night
And never any rioting.

I have a friendship,
With all the people in the world,
No free trade,
Fair trade and the time of our lives.

I have faith,
All the races come together,
Join to make one
And live in peace.

I have a miracle,
It shows all,
We can be faithful and true,
But to never turn our back.

I have a dream,
Do you have a dream?
I hope everyone has a dream,
It's a magnificent thing!

Hannah Rhodes (14)
Norwich High School for Girls, Norwich

The View From My Cell

Where are you going to be in ten years time?
Will you be happy with the way you have been living your life?
I have a vision,
I have a thought,
I am on a mission,
It is just how I've been taught.

I will change this world,
I will change my life,
I will be the one to make it alright,
I will make it pure,
I will make it better,
I will be the one and only creator.

Living in this world where people are dying, sighing and crying,
There is no innocence, there are no dreams,
I lie awake at night, trying to fall asleep,
I shut my eyes trying to dream,
Thinking of good thoughts, without being mean.

Looking through the windows with the wrought iron bars,
Staring in the darkness, looking at my scars,
I wish I had not done that evil little thing,
I wish I had not committed that awful, awful sin.

Why am I here, in this filthy rotten cell?
Is there no hope, no immortal soul?
I thought I had changed, obviously not,
I am still stuck with this name, warped in a knot.

I will never be free,
Perhaps, I will die of insanity,
I will try and fall asleep and reach the land of nod,
Maybe if I'm good, one day I'll be with God.

Maybe, maybe, I will try and live in hope,
Maybe, maybe, I will live and cope!

Sophia Thompson (14)
Norwich High School for Girls, Norwich

I Have A Dream

Whilst my head rest soundly on my pillow,
Many heads in Africa did not.

Last night,
Whilst I lay comfortably dreaming,
Many minds in Africa could not.

Last night,
My mind was filled with messages,
My eyes were opened when every politician's were closed.

I swept high above the plains of Africa,
A stream of tears trickling down my face,
For before me lay what had been born only in imaginative minds.

Clean water trickled freely into empty buckets,
Accompanied by happy voices,
Which burst from smiling faces.

Flowing, glistening, pure, *safe* water,
Was swallowed longingly,
By those who needed it.

Gleaming, hygenic, pristine medical instruments,
Lay on top of a surgical green sterilised sheet,
Whilst a patient received urgent treatment.

Happy smiles,
Gleamed on young faces,
As *free* children played on the riverbank.

This had been many people's dream,
Such a simple one,
Yet it is *still* only a dream.

Natalie Bayton (12)
Norwich High School for Girls, Norwich

I Have A Dream

I n the future, wouldn't you like to live in a world that is fair?

H ave men and women receiving equal pay
A nd being respected for what we achieve,
not be judged according to our looks,
V ast countries choose women by appearance, in this modern day
E ast communities, however, seem to have overcome this though.

A dapting to a certain strategy of eliminating this discrimination -
The Hajabb.

D rowning out this unfair democracy,
R espect their customs and praise their ideas,
maybe it is time we are influenced by their ways,
Don't you think it would be for the good?
Why is it always us westerners that show the way?
E veryone is born with an innerself,
Don't you think we should use it and not hide it away?
This is truthfully our natural beauty.
A mazing thoughts and discoveries,
M ade through us understanding our innerselves.

Marie Mallinder (14)
Norwich High School for Girls, Norwich

I Have A Dream Of The World

Spices fill the air, and tickle your nose,
Snow-tipped mountains tower above you,
Doughnut and burger bars fill the city,
Zebras, rhinos and lions cover the open land,
Surfers and swimmers scatter the giant waves,
A country smothered in a while blanket of snow,
These beautiful scenes cover the Earth,
I wish that they will stay forever
And that one day I will visit them all
And so many other beautiful places.

Alice Whitehead (11)
Norwich High School for Girls, Norwich

If I Were To Paint The World

If I were to paint over the world,
Change the mood completely,
I'd paint it white and baby blue,
Pale pink and yellow too.
Colours of happiness, freedom and joy,
Colours of peace and love,
Colours of humility,
Generous colours,
Colours of tranquillity,
Considerate colours,
Colours of equality,
Truthful colours,
Colours of harmony,
Beautiful colours.

Jane Shaker (11)
Norwich High School for Girls, Norwich

I Have A Dream

I have a dream,
That it will always seem,
That we are all equal in God's eyes,
It won't matter,
If we chatter,
To people who are black and white,
We won't get in a fright,
Or even turn away,
If we hear someone say,
'Oh that black model looks nice,'
If we do, we are all mice,
Because it's what's inside that counts.

Rosie Cooke (11)
Norwich High School for Girls, Norwich

I Have A Dream

In my dream, money grows on trees,
Animals can talk and sing,
The entire world wants peace,
Peace instead of anything.

In my dream, all water is clean,
There is no such thing as poverty,
Everyone is nice and never mean,
All humans are totally free.

In my dream, everywhere is joyful,
No faces are looking glum,
The entire nation is always loyal,
People talking about their best chum.

In my dream, hope is all around,
All trees and plants grow strong,
Anything that is lost is quickly found,
Moments of joy are long.

In my dream, love is always there,
Kisses and hugs to cheer up the sad,
Tending each and everywhere,
No one has ever been bad.

In my dream, everyone is rich,
If someone is poor, we share,
No one is left lying in a ditch,
This is the way to show you care.

Olivia Martin (11)
Norwich High School for Girls, Norwich

I Have A Dream

I have a dream of a rainbow-covered sky,
Of sun-dashed hills and larks soaring high,
Of rain-filled clouds and foggy days,
Of snow-capped mountains in a misty haze.

I have a dream of sun-dappled sands,
Where clear blue waves reach out like hands,
Where palm trees sway in the gentle breeze,
Where fishing boats bob on the azure seas.

I have a dream of snow-topped hills,
Of pounding waterfalls gushing over the mills,
Of children stamping in puddles deep,
Of shepherds patiently tending their sheep.

I have a dream, a nightmare, it's true,
Where drought and famine spoil the view,
Where envy, hatred, fear and pain,
Where people are dying like a fading flame.

I have a dream that a time will come,
Of peace on Earth for everyone,
Of happiness, hope, health and love,
Of all that is good, gliding down like a dove.

Camilla Le Coq (12)
Norwich High School for Girls, Norwich

I Have A Dream

I have a dream that one day the world will live in peace,
Which means, no war, no fights, no guns.

I have a dream that one day there will be no poverty,
Which means, no hunger, no poor, no homeless.

I have a dream that one day everyone will be equal,
Which means, no racism, but peace between religions and colours.

I have a dream that one day there will be no global warming,
Which means, no harmful gases, but beautiful white winters.

I have a dream that one day the world will be its beautiful old self,
Which means, no litter, no pollution and all the natural things.

As you can see, I want a lot,
But it gets to this, the world will be a better,
Brighter and much safer place!

Kelly Hunter (12)
Norwich High School for Girls, Norwich

Together As One - Haikus

I have a vision
The world is a perfect place
Unharmed all over.

There is no violence
Unhappiness and distress
Do not exist here.

People are as one
Playing together this day
Happy as can be.

One day I believe
This world of mine will exist,
God's children as one.

Hetty Stephen (12)
Norwich High School for Girls, Norwich

I Have A Dream

When the world is perfect,
I will be . . .
An angel for
Eternity.

                I'll make the rivers
                Flow so free,
                They won't run dry,
                They'll reach the sea.

I'll make the mountains,
As high as can be,
There won't be any
Poverty.

                I'll make all illnesses,
                Go from thee,
                It won't be there,
                It won't, you'll see.

This is my dream,
It's full of glee,
Join me and I will
Set you free.

                What would life be
                Like without
                Dreams?

Pippa Jones (11)
Norwich High School for Girls, Norwich

I Dream Of A Life Of Peace And Happiness For Everybody

The ripples of a bubbling brook,
Beneath the shady trees,
The golden coloured corn,
Swaying in the breeze.

The hens with their newborn chicks,
Basking in the sun,
The bark of an excited dog,
Out to have some fun.

The tempting smell of baking bread,
Wafting through the air,
The sight of plump, red strawberries,
Soon for us to share.

The sweet scent of summer flowers,
Their heads held in the sun,
Exotic coloured butterflies,
Passing by them, one by one.

The sound of a cricket ball,
Bouncing off a bat,
The shouts from the players,
'Howzat!'

Brightly coloured roses
And apples on the trees,
Sweet, amber honey,
Freshly made by the bees.

A life like that would be fabulous but others are still
Trying to find hope in themselves to fulfil their dreams.

The cold and loneliness of a shack,
Where people have to live,
Why is it them and why not us?
Who is it they'll never forgive?

The rumbling of their tummies,
Praying for just a little to eat,
When we can snack all day through
And fill our stomachs with nice hot meat.

Out that night, all cold and tired,
Sleeping rough on the hard, damp ground,
When we are curled up in our cosy beds,
Fast asleep safe and sound.

On the streets, life is no fun,
People are begging, all night and day,
We are living our lives to the full,
How come we got to live the right way?

Lucy Temple (12)
Norwich High School for Girls, Norwich

My Dream - Haikus

If I had a dream
I'd make world peace forever
No guns, no nothing.

If I had a dream
I would make a perfect world
With lots of chocolate.

If I had a dream
There would be not one worry
There'd be no sorrow.

If I had a dream
No illness to scorch the world
We would be happy.

If I had a dream
There would be no racism
Everyone's equal.

If I had a dream
There'd be happiness throughout
Our treacherous world.

Milly Larner (11)
Norwich High School for Girls, Norwich

I Have A Dream

All the hills and earth are bursting with song,
Grass is green and lush, with flowers in bloom,
Trees are swaying in a fresh, fragrant breeze,
The sky is clear blue and birds fill the sky,
The world is content with itself for now.

No flowers bloom and tree stumps try to grow,
The sky is dark, and shows thunder clouds forming,
The birds have fled, no longer singing a tune,
Is this our future on Earth to be?
I have a dream to cut down pollution,
To stamp it out and find more solutions!

Rachael Hopley (11)
Norwich High School for Girls, Norwich

I Have A Dream

(This poem was written in memory of Martin Luther King who was an inspiration to us all)

'I have a dream,'
Is what a famous man once said,
With his words that shook the world,
That was now full of dread!

His words full of meaning,
He spoke full of power,
His posture tall and strong,
He was now the man of the hour.

Who was to know,
On that fateful day,
Someone would be shot,
They should have never taken him away.

But 37 years on,
He is still living,
In my heart and in yours,
Even in death, he is giving.

Jessica Beattie (12)
Norwich High School for Girls, Norwich

What A Polar Bear Thinks

I sit here every day,
Thinking about the time,
When people will have to pay,
For stepping too far out of line.

They're melting my home,
Slowly, bit by bit,
They're too lazy to walk,
In their cars they sit.

Why don't they see,
That they are ruining the globe?
If they turned off their TV's,
Then there may be some hope.

Why don't they stop,
Before it's too late?
We need their help
And don't have time to wait.

Hatty Ekbery (11)
Norwich High School for Girls, Norwich

My Dream For A Better World

Last night I had a dream,
That the world became a better place,
It all followed a happy theme
And sadness was banished from everyone's face.

No more famine, no more war,
No more drought, no more crime,
Peace and harmony, we want more!
Love and happiness all the time.

Kill the cancers, stop the bombs,
End the poverty and all the abuse,
I dreamt that the entire world got on,
Being nasty is not an excuse.

Tamzin Steggles (11)
Norwich High School for Girls, Norwich

I Have A Dream

Open fields filled with hopping bunnies,
Ewes looking after their precious young lambs,
Snorting pigs rooting through their food filled troughs.

Red brick farmhouses selling warm, fresh bread,
Cleanly swept stables, just for milking cows,
Boxes of fragile eggs, six to a pack!

I knead the gooey, sticky dough with glee!
My hands all covered, all icky and nice,
Sliding the fresh bread off the baking tray.

Empty, deserted, collapsed old mud huts,
No sign of life in any of the trees,
A world of loneliness waiting to die.

Dry, crumpled plants drooping in the boiling heat,
Any chance of income gone, 'oh' too soon,
A dry summer causing rumbling tummies.

Hot, feverish, young children are in pain,
No money to call for a caring nurse,
Minds slowly drifting away from this life.

Could poverty possibly be any worse?
Could country life be any happier?

Elizabeth Bamber (11)
Norwich High School for Girls, Norwich

I Have A Dream That . . .

I have a dream that . . .
There will be world peace always,
No fighting, no wars.

I have a dream that . . .
There is a chocolate fountain,
In my back garden.

I have a dream that . . .
One day we won't compare others
And always be as one.

I have a dream that . . .
The sun will always be shining
And drown out sadness.

I have a dream that . . .
No matter what we believe,
We won't be punished.

I have a dream that . . .
Sweets and chocolate grow on trees,
Take it when we want!

I dream lots of things . . .
But only some things come true,
So keep on dreaming!

Aimi Eagle (11)
Norwich High School for Girls, Norwich

I Have A Dream

I have a dream, a dream of peace,
A smile on every face, even laughter,
Forgetting old differences and singing together,
Let us sing of love, of hope and of peace,
Let us open our eyes and see the world in a new way,
Beneath all the treachery, there is paradise.

I have a dream, a dream of love,
Feeling love of those you don't even know,
Lay down your weapons and burn then,
Burn them with your hate,
Think of the lives that would've been spared,
The blood that has been spilt,
Because we are so blind,
Think of the brothers, fathers, sons, mothers and sisters,
The families that have been torn apart,
Imagine the broad smiles it would bring,
To have a world without war, without hate.

Laura Butters (12)
Norwich High School for Girls, Norwich

A Better World

I f I had a perfect world

H urricanes and tornadoes would not hit America
A laska's ice would not be melting,
V olcanoes would not erupt,
E arthquakes would not make people homeless

A cid rain would not be caused by driving cars

D rinking water would be clean for everyone
R ising sea levels would not flood coastlines
E nemies would not go to war
A ll children would go to school
M ore people would take care of their environment.

Georgina Rhead (12)
Norwich High School for Girls, Norwich

I Had A Dream . . .

I was running down the cold empty street,
All I could hear was the thud of my heartbeat,
I was lonely and sad and nobody cared,
Could I go back to school tomorrow
And should I be scared?
I tucked into the corner, and hid in the shadows,
Waited till darkness when there were no fellows,
When I get home, all is terribly black,
Why is it I feel like I have a devil on my back?
I turn around and swiftly walk to the door,
I see you standing there and the next thing
I knew, I fell to the floor,
Why did I be the one to be bullied by you?
What have I ever said to you or done?
I'm only a kid, and I'm still young.

The next morning, when I finally awoke,
I thought to myself, *that wasn't a joke,*
People out there are having that happen to them every day
And the people that do that should have to pay,
For everyone needs a chance in life,
To show you that they're OK and you think twice!

Sammy Haycox (11)
Norwich High School for Girls, Norwich

Peace

P erfect life like a flowing calm ocean,
E arth is safe as a healthy, bright red apple,
A life is even, no rich, poor or enemies,
C herish the humans, black or white,
E nter a world that makes others happy.

Madi Brown (12)
Norwich High School for Girls, Norwich

I Have A Dream

Steaming soup in the bowl, before your eyes,
Warming up your cold hands before the fire,
The hot food passes your lips and runs down,
The joy of sleeping in a comfy bed,
Memories of being out on the streets,
Wake up happy, you know you've got a friend,
Have breakfast and shower, have some fun,
Stay at home, enjoy all the comfort leisures.

You could put these things in other people's lives,
Make a big difference to someone's life.

Victoria Proctor (11)
Norwich High School for Girls, Norwich

Hope

Yesterday I ate my dinner and wondered,
How come I get all this lovely food,
When some people in Africa have none at all?
I thought about this again and again,
What difference can I make in this world?
All I can do is hope for the very best,
I wish that years after me, they will have hope,
That they will have a dream to continue life,
That they will have a warm dinner each day,
But most of all I have hope for them, so
That in generations to come, food will be there
And a caring heart for each and every one,
There are many things that could be changed in this world.
If we can't change everything, then start with hope,
If they believe, then hope will come into their hearts,
Hope is a little thing that can make a big difference,
Hope is the gift that everyone has.

Katie Ackers (12)
Norwich High School for Girls, Norwich

I Have A Dream

In a shack with a wooden floor that creaks,
Some children shiver helplessly nearby,
This scene pictures poverty at its peak,
Let us put an end to this suffering.
Just look at their houses, aren't they bleak?
With only a chair and crumbling walls,
This pig is dying and their roof leaks,
What have they done to deserve this treatment?
And who are the 'they' I keep mentioning?
We all know that it's not just in one country, I mean.

Mary Wheeler (11)
Norwich High School for Girls, Norwich

The Rainforest

A luscious green haven bursting with life,
A nearby waterfall glistens,
In the sunlight, shining through the tall trees.

The call of a cockatoo far away,
The sparkling dew drops on the long wild grass,
An unspoilt, untouched world on its own.

But then they strike, those monsters with their saws,
No good heart, just mindless munching machines,
I tell them to leave but I'm just a child,
They laugh and they chant, cigars in their mouths.

Tears fill my eyes; I'm helpless and alone,
I long for an adult to brainwash them,
But no one is in sight, it is barren.

My dream is that one day, destruction will stop,
The 'lungs of the Earth' will be fully restored
And the Earth will live in peace once again.

Helen Baxter (11)
Norwich High School for Girls, Norwich

I Had A Dream

It is all your fault I went to bed scared
And dreamt you followed me everywhere,
I could hear your footsteps constantly there,
You followed me, taunted me, you scared me.
I couldn't escape at school, vulnerable,
You pushed me and I couldn't get away,
I see you and run but you shout after,
Your voice is left ringing inside my head,
You're the reason I missed school yesterday,
But I dreamt otherwise, deep in my sleep.

You weren't there, I was free to walk the streets,
I wasn't cowering in the corner,
I wasn't scared to leave the house today,
Because you wouldn't be waiting for me,
You wouldn't be waiting at the corner,
Not ready to ruin my day, my life,
I could stand freely, out of the corner,
Hold my head up higher than yesterday,
It was bliss not to think, not aware,
Of the dangers facing me tomorrow.

Alice Rickett (12)
Norwich High School for Girls, Norwich

I Have A Dream

A wild stallion runs as free as the wind,
The desert is spread out in front of him,
He knows he is very lucky to be free,
Very far away, across the oceans,
An Indian child sits knotting carpets,
She really longs to be free and have rights,
She is a slave and has no choice at all,
Every person in the world should be free,
I have a dream that everyone is free
And everyone is treated equally.

Eleanor Stanley (12)
Norwich High School for Girls, Norwich

War

The booming sound of deadly bombs, falling,
Crashing to the ground,
Now lives they owe,
The *booming* hearts of innocent children,
A frightened wife, now a frightened widow.

What is the cause of these *booming* events?
I dream of a world full of peace,
But how can one small being change the world today,
When the real power is locked, safe?

It will take something as powerful as a bomb to change the world,
Boom!
A brave man needs to be that bomb,
To change the minds of the human race,
Which is unaware, it is open to doom.

It must soon stop, as friends are decreasing
And enemies are preparing to fight,
It must stop, as countries are dying
And soon the whole world will be *booming* with fright.

Mary Peart (13)
Norwich High School for Girls, Norwich

I Had A Dream

African children laugh with happiness,
They're smiling and waving with all their joy,
There is no more poverty or hunger.

Lots of water falling from up above,
They have safe fresh water all around them,
No need for any more children to die.

Fresh food cooking, a nice dinner tonight!
Warming all the people's cold tummies up,
They will have no more bugs or diseases,
All treated equally, no more Third World.

Charlotte Randle (11)
Norwich High School for Girls, Norwich

Cloaked Life

We are undiscovered; see us, the rainbow that hides,
Not a cloud in the sky, not that we see,
The great red giants block out all sunlight,
No sky, no clouds, no blues or bright white light,
Just green and brown.

We are undiscovered, leave us,
We lived in darkness,
Covered by our shroud,
An old woman with a shawl,
Dark heavy colours, mysterious and protective,
Yet bursting with life and sounds.

We are undiscovered, help us,
A closely weaved web,
Slashed by strobes,
Let it stay,
Untouched,
Like blades of grass, reborn.

We are undiscovered, sense us,
You cannot catch us, touch us, see us or smell us,
But we are here,
We are wisps in the glossy green shade,
Vanishing like crude magic acts.

We were undiscovered, save us,
When Man and roar came in,
Found and pushed, long gone are we,
Our homes and dreams alike.

We were undiscovered, forget us,
As emptiness rolls and ground turns to dust,
Old ways forgotten, new ways fail,
We shall not help the devils of land.

It was undiscovered, nurture it,
Want to go back, can't go back,
To what there used to be,
New, big sky, fat clouds, smooth blues and bright white light.

We are discovered, learn from us,
Gentle and simple, guide you we must,
Sneered you did, our sounds falter, and melt.
Yet I have a dream that I can go back,
Than man and roar will leave and nurture it,
Old life dead, salvation possibly,
Resuscitation, begged. Earth as ashes parched.

I have a dream,
Green darkness, resume,
Covering like a shroud,
An old woman with a shawl,
Dark heavy colours, mysterious and protective,
Yet bursting with life and sounds,
Learn from us.
Gentle and simply. Guide you we must,
Land and sound knit together, a sock old but mended.

I have that dream, let me share it, let others follow it,
Let dust re-gather and life heal.
Retreat, and safe will existence be.

Katherine Furniss (13)
Norwich High School for Girls, Norwich

I Have A Dream

My sight is obscured by wet, warm, green leaves,
I come to a clearing and I can see,
Exotic flowers and a waterfall,
Crashing down into a turquoise blue pool.

I hear the buzzing of unique insects,
The tinkling water, I never forget,
The smell of pollen and undergrowth green,
My perfect world finished with a gleam,
Something like this, I would love to have seen,
This solitary paradise, my dream.

Millie Farrant (12)
Norwich High School for Girls, Norwich

I Have A Dream

Sleek fur glistening magnificently in the sun,
Baby cubs playing happily, having fun,
A long tail flopped lazily on the ground,
Laying slightly raised on a small delicate mound.

Hidden, camouflaged up a tree,
Watching the world go by, from here everything she can see,
With her kill she bravely fought for and got,
She rests, eats her fill not likely to stop.

I dream of tracking these magnificent animals,
Watching their every move,
Treating them if they're hurt or ill,
Watching as they learn to kill.

She is a lion, she is a queen,
Of the jungle, I have seen,
But still she's always fighting for her life,
From the poachers, from the gun, from the knife.

They want her for her beautiful skin,
What do they think she is? Just a thing,
She frantically runs trying to hide,
But she knows she's been got already inside.

This is the end, the end of her run,
She lies there whimpering in the sun,
Her cubs all around her, wondering what's going on,
Then they realise that their mummy's gone.

They run away with tears in their eyes,
The man with the gun has ruined their lives,
They dare to look back and
See their precious mum all tied up in a sack.

They know there's no hope for them now too,
They're too young to survive, they're too new,
With a whole life ahead of them, a world to explore,
The man with the gun has just slammed shut the door.

Rebecca Wooldridge (11)
Norwich High School for Girls, Norwich

I Have A Dream

I have a dream that poverty and hunger will be no more.
Neither will misery, children will be laughing and playing happily,
Proper houses and happy families.

No more walking miles for water,
Dying at a young age will not happen,
People will live a long and happy life,
Food won't cost as much and people won't starve.

People should be able to afford food
So they won't starve,
We should help these people,
There should be no more poverty or hunger,
That is my dream that I would like to have.

I would like to help crack down on poverty.

Brontë Goodwin (11)
Norwich High School for Girls, Norwich

The End Of Greed

My bounty of an empire, bleeding dry once more,
Just because the rich were selfish
And wouldn't give to the poor.

Sadness upon my windowpane,
Death approaching my door, all because I was greedy
And wanted more.

We can put a stop to this,
Whether rich or poor,
We will all put a stop to this,
So we all can live in total bliss.

Sasha Baynham (11)
Norwich High School for Girls, Norwich

The Tiny Question

If people didn't have it in them,
If no one could physically fight,
If people would only agree,
If we weren't seen in black or white.

Then every bit of war would be over,
There wouldn't be a good reason to fight,
Everyone would agree with each other,
No one would care if we were black or white.

Picture a world filled with peace and love,
Where there isn't a single sign of a fight,
Where everyone is free to speak their minds
And you can be friends with *black and white*.

If the smell of death wasn't in the air,
If TV's didn't always show a fight,
If people could just trust each other,
Then we wouldn't be seen in black or white.

Why do people think it all matters?
War, people dying, killing in a fight,
Is this the best way to settle things?
Sometimes over if we're black or white.

If you think that's the way to move on,
That world peace will come in a fight,
Then just ask yourself a tiny question,
Do you really care if we're black or white?

Ellen Kirby (13)
Norwich High School for Girls, Norwich

The Last Bullet

The last plane has flown over,
The last gunshot fired,
The last person's life has been taken,
The last man has been killed,
The slaughter was at last ceased.

A scary silence takes over, but
A new sound steals the silence,
A sound of laughter and happiness,
A sound of survivors that live on,
A sense of joy fills the air.

The war should never have begun,
The lives should not have been lost,
The beautiful land should not have been torn by war,
The blood should not have flowed,
The bullets should not have been shot.

A dream for you would be 'no war',
A dream that no innocent lives were lost,
A dream that there was no conflict,
A dream of a war-free land,
A land without a shot.

The land, not a swamp, but a flowery field,
The land peaceful, not noisy with gunshots,
The land with everyone holding hands,
The land where everyone is content,
All peaceful, with love engulfing us all.

Rachel Mumford (13)
Norwich High School for Girls, Norwich

No More War

No more war,
Silence, silence in the air,
Silence, silence everywhere,
Not a sound to be heard,
Not a shot to be fired,
You could hear the crackle of a fire.

I sensed the song before I heard it,
The clean calm happiness,
Coming from every voice
And yes, in the middle of the many men,
Stood a crackling fire.

Huge grey weapons,
Being chucked fiercely on
And crackling and burning,
To hoots of laughter,
Not to mention song.

Two sides, two countries,
Sitting around a fire,
Holding hands, singing a song,
Smiling, laughing,
All thoughts of war forgotten.

I have a dream,
Of the end of war,
But it is just a fantasy,
I want it to be reality,
This is my hope for tomorrow.

Rosie Vavasour (12)
Norwich High School for Girls, Norwich

Peace

Burn, guns, burn,
Your death will save many people,
Burn, fire, burn,
Eat up the hatred in the world,
The evil will be gone in this Earth,
So that there will only be peace.

Fly, dove, fly,
Spread your happiness across the land,
Shine, light, shine,
Bring the world some peace and hope,
Abolish darkness, evil and hatred,
So that there will only be peace.

Sing, people, sing,
Show everyone how much joy you have,
Pray, man, pray,
Pray for a life of hope,
Make sure your life is joyful,
All the way through,
Make sure that there is peace,
Peace,
And only peace.

Jess Collinson (12)
Norwich High School for Girls, Norwich

Famine

Imagine:
No food, no clean water, the feeling of starvation,
The feeling that you're going to be sick, you're going to die,
Begging on dirty, dusty floors for anything anyone will give you,
Ribs sticking out, no flesh or fat, just bones.

All because you don't have any food.

I have a dream that the starving would not be the starving anymore,
That they could eat like we can,
Freely whatever they want,
No groans but laughter.
Just the munching and crunching as they eat,
No tummies rumbling for food, just a smile
On their faces showing, 'thank you'!
I dream that they could run freely through beautiful corn fields,
Their hair blowing in the wind,
Pick an apple from a tree
And just start nibbling into it,
Slurp clean water from a fountain, and feel it drop
Down their mouths.

Just think if we could do something to help them,
The smiles and laughter that would come and never go,
Well maybe we can . . .

Lucy Hardy (13)
Norwich High School for Girls, Norwich

I Had A Dream - The Rainforest

I had a dream of redwoods in all their glory,
I could smell the fragrance of the blooms in the scrub,
I had a dream of birds of vibrant colour,
I could hear the chatter of the monkeys,
I had a dream, skies tropical, sea blue,
I could taste the mangos, lush and ripe,
I had a dream, rivers of exotic curious fish,
I had a nightmare, the roar of an army of diggers, advancing,
I could smell the burning of the redwood,
I had a nightmare, the human destruction,
I could hear the gnawing of chainsaws,
I had a nightmare, animals frightened, alone and starving!
I caould taste toxic petrol fumes,
I had a nightmare, nests, lairs and burrows destroyed,
I prefer dreaming, let's save our rainforest,
Because it will not return!

Sara-Jayne Williams (13)
Norwich High School for Girls, Norwich

My Dream

I am going to be a jet pilot,
I dream of going 500 miles an hour,
Of being above the clouds,
Clouds as white as snow,
Like cotton wool spread over the land,
I will travel around the world,
See different places and people
And make new friends.

Luke Sewell (12)
Reepham High School, Norwich

My Thoughts

My little brother is concerned about global warming,
It is always in the news,
He worries, *will we all drown if the ice caps melt?*
My mum says it won't happen in our day.

My nan and grandad live in France,
Bird flu has just been discovered there,
Now they won't eat chicken in case it is infected.

If the weather would just warm up to spring,
We would be able to play in the park,
It would keep us active and healthy,
A skate park in Reepham would keep us all fit.

Sometimes I dream I play for Man Utd,
I am saving goals against Chelsea,
We are top of the Premiership
And heading for Europe.

In my garden I would like my own shed,
In it I will hold Warhammer tournaments,
It will be a special clubhouse,
I will battle against my little brother.

Liam Waller (12)
Reepham High School, Norwich

I Have A Dream

I dream of owning my own dog,
A little Jack Russell,
I will walk it,
Feed it,
Love it,
He will protect me
And help me exercise!
He will keep mecompany,
That would be my dream.

Carla Woodcock (11)
Reepham High School, Norwich

I Have A Dream

I have a dream,
Of somewhere where everyone has friends,
Somewhere calm, quiet and peaceful,
But that is only a dream.

I have a dream,
Of a place where there are no drugs,
No alcohol and fags,
But that is only a dream.

I have a dream,
Where there are no fights, no wars
And everyone is at peace,
But that is only a dream.

I have a dream,
Where everyone has a home,
There are no children's homes needed
And there isn't any homeless people out on the streets,
But that is only a dream.

I have one more dream,
Where all of these dreams are real
And everyone is happy in a better world,
This is only a dream but hopefully
It will become true!

Helen Betts (12)
Reepham High School, Norwich

I Have A Dream

I am going to be a wonderful actress,
I'll be the princess in the pantomime,
Brad Pitt will be my leading man,
I'll go to Hollywood
And make some films,
I'll make my handprint on Hollywood Boulevard,
I will live my dream.

Eryn Kirkcaldy (11)
Reepham High School, Norwich

I Have A Dream

I dream of being a racing driver,
I'll race banger cars,
Crash, bang, squeal, screech!
My car will be dented and scratched,
The crowd will cheer for me,
Shouting, roaring and clapping,
Mine will be the last car running,
The winner.

Oliver Rayner (12)
Reepham High School, Norwich

I Have A Dream

I dream of living under the sea,
I won't be scared, it's safe,
I'll clean the shark's teeth,
I'll eat fish and seaweed,
I'll live in a big bubble
And will be able to see,
All the creatures outside,
I dream of talking to the animals.

Jack Wardle (12)
Reepham High School, Norwich

My Dream

I dream of going into space,
I'll go up in a rocket,
Flames shooting out,
Speeding towards the stars,
Twinkling in the pitch-black sky,
Peaceful, quiet, alone,
I dream of planets, strange and unusual,
But I think it's just a dream.

Vicki Giles (12)
Reepham High School, Norwich

My Dream

I love cars, all cars, lots of cars,
I love speed, I dream of racing,
Racing on a track,
Brands Hatch, the Nurbergring,
I dream of presenting 'Top Gear'
Testing cars and beating
Jeremy Clarkson!
That's my dream!

Jake Pearce (11)
Reepham High School, Norwich

I Have A Dream

I dream of a peaceful world,
There will be no wars,
People will not worry about
The colour of your skin,
Terrorists won't abuse others,
Children will be safe,
This should be everybody's dream.

Bradley Graves (11)
Reepham High School, Norwich

I Have A Dream

Medicine is my dream,
I want to be a paramedic,
I will be able to help people,
I'll drive an ambulance,
I'll have my sirens blasting
And the blue lights flashing,
I'll drive fast through red lights,
If I have to . . .
I'll try to save lives,
My dream will come true.

Rosie Feltham (12)
Reepham High School, Norwich

I Have A Dream

I love motorbikes,
I'm going to have one,
I'm going to be a champion.

That's my dream,
It will be a blue bike,
As blue as blueberries,
It will be 1000cc
The speed of light.

That's my dream.

Christopher Forrest (11)
Reepham High School, Norwich

I Have A Dream

I dream of singing with Robbie Williams,
We'll stand together on the stage,
The crowd will cheer us,
The cameras film us,
We're on TV,
We'll make CDs,
I'll be famous
And Robbie will be mine,
In my dreams.

Megan Watling (12)
Reepham High School, Norwich

I Have A Dream

I have a dream that's inside my head,
I have a dream of someone dead,
In the world there are people dying,
Can't you hear the non-stop crying?
Do something to help today,
Don't turn your back and run away.

Deanna Cooper (12)
Reepham High School, Norwich

I Have A Dream

In my dreams, I see a pink giraffe made out of candy,
But some people don't even know what candy is,
Why is life so unfair?

In my dreams there is a happy place,
Where no one is hungry,
But some places don't even have much food.

In my dreams I see lots of children,
But in some places there are hardly any children,
Why is life so unfair?

In my dreams, I think of where I like to live, do you?

Sarah Roberts (12)
Reepham High School, Norwich

I Have A Dream

I have a dream,
That one day the world will be a better place,
No litter, no waste, no pollution,
Everyone will live a simple life,
No roads, no vehicles, no accidents.
The world will live without any limits,
No walls, no gates, no prisons,
Everyone will be able to live without fear,
No bullies, no wars, no violence.
The world will live in peace and harmony, together,
No sadness, no crying, no anger!
Everyone will have a family,
None abandoned, none neglected, none abused,
To be equal, no matter what or whom you are,
No racists, no judges,
Everyone has a voice,
No silence.
I have a dream that one day,
This will become a reality.

Louise Bugg (12)
Reepham High School, Norwich

Bad Dreams, Good Dreams

Bad dreams are:
People living in poverty,
Drugs,
Bullies and the bullied,
Natural disasters,
These are what we all want to get
Better or stopped.

Good dreams are:
Having more money, so people
Don't have to work,
Having nice hot holidays,
More shops to buy things in.

But how come people are more interested,
In the things they want, and money
And are not interested in making
The bad things better?

Chloe Dunton (11)
Reepham High School, Norwich

I Have A Dream

I have a dream to always fly,
I have a dream to never die.

I have a dream to play for City,
I have a dream to live for infinity.

I have a dream to smell forever,
I had a dream to be made of leather.

I have a dream to swim like a fish,
I have a dream to grant you a wish.

I have a dream to be like a bear,
I have a dream to live in a lair.

I have a dream to be a bird that sings,
I have a dream to do all of these things.

Henry Skinner (11)
Reepham High School, Norwich

I Have A Dream

If I could I would stop poverty,
I would let children have food,
A place to live,
To be loved.

If I had the power, I would stop the trees from
Getting pulled down,
So squirrels and birds will live there.

If I could I would have a pet,
A dog,
A cat,
Anything would do for me.

If I had the power I would have a nicer brother
And he would be kind to me.

If I could I would have magic powers,
I would harness the weather,
No tsunamis,
No floods
And no mud slides
And everyone will live in peace.

Sophie Speer (12)
Reepham High School, Norwich

I Had A Dream

I had a dream . . .
And in that dream,
All poverty was transformed into
Wealth and kindness,
All disease carrying bugs and animals
Were killed and made extinct,
All wars were stopped and peace was made
And all yobs and vandals were sent to prison
And became caring citizens of their country.

Nick Davis (11)
Reepham High School, Norwich

It's A Nasty World Out There

No more murders,
No more wars,
Why can't this all stop? I hate it!
Children screaming,
Children scared,
Bullets firing,
Burning buildings,
Hearts broken, help me, help us all,
Why can't this all stop? I hate it!

No more poverty,
No more hunger,
Why can't this all stop? I hate it!
Flies on faces,
Stomachs swollen,
Ribs showing,
Families frantic,
Hearts broken, help me, help us all,
Why can't this all stop? I hate it!

No more kidnaps,
No more abuse,
Why can't this all stop? I hate it!
Suicide bombers,
Destroyed futures,
Lives wasted,
Lives lost,
Hearts broken, help me, help us all,
Why can't this all stop? I hate it!
So stop now!

Polly Randell-Bateman (12)
Reepham High School, Norwich

My Dream

I wish that in the world things would change,
The poverty, the fighting, the hurt and the blame.

Norfolk would be better and nicer,
If only my mobile could get a signal,
I could ring my mum and say 'I'm safe, see you later.'
If the sun would just shine on my school holidays,
So many more days out for us all to enjoy.

There are many things, not great just small,
That I'd like to change -
Having my own bedroom,
Is just one thing,
The poor and under privileged getting a little more.

To make our world a much better place,
My dreams that I have mentioned,
I can change a few with some help, just some,
But together - who knows - what we could all do.

Becky Manton (12)
Reepham High School, Norwich

I Had A Vision

I had a vision that the war was over,
I had a vision that the whole world shook
Lands and no one ever fought again,
I had a vision that everyone who had done
Something wrong, turned themselves in,
I had a vision that all the taxes went down,
I had a vision that everyone was safe
And no one could get hurt,
I had a vision that education was free,
I had a vision that all crime was stopped,
I had a vision that no one was in danger,
Everyone was safe.

Michaela Crane (11)
Reepham High School, Norwich

I Once Dreamt . . .

I once dreamt that there was no poverty
And that disease was a thing of the past,
World peace was finally not a dream, but reality,
Dictatorship was blown away in the wind,
World disasters were a glimmer on the horizon
And environmental issues were overcome.

I once dreamt that it was no longer a hard life for elderly people
And entertainment for teens kept them out of trouble,
A cinema and go-kart track are the little things,
But a town hall would be good too.

I once dreamt I had a little more money for me and for you
And better jobs for my parents
And a little more money would be pretty nice too,
A bigger house would be within my reach
And more friends, as you can never have too many.

I once dreamt that I would make my friends and
                family eternally happy,
And be able to control time, to do all the things you never
Get time to do, to travel in space, with no restrictions,
I once dreamt I would make the most of my life . . .
But that I intend to do!

Jordan McDowall (12)
Reepham High School, Norwich

I Have A Dream

I would make sure that all the poor people had money,
So that they are not poor anymore,
I wouldn't have any wars because people get hurt,
I would like to stop the bird flu, so no more birds die
Or any more people,
Because people and birds are dying from it,
I think that we can stop people getting murdered,
I dream that no animals are killed.

Emma Osborne (11)
Reepham High School, Norwich

Make It Happen

You can stop poverty, if you make it happen,
You can share water all around the world, If you make it happen,
You can help families by giving your old clothes to charity,
You can make it happen.

You can change our Prime Minister,
You can make it happen,
You can provide clubs for the young and old people,
You can help people get around easier,
Only if you make it happen.

You can make it happen,
You can help people with illnesses,
You can make your ambitions come true,
You can make wishes,
You can make it happen.

Sophie Maddox (11)
Reepham High School, Norwich

I Have A Dream . . .

I have a dream that all the illnesses in the world
Would be banished in the blink of an eye,
I have a dream that all war would stop,
As quickly as a cobra strikes,
I have a dream that all people could be treated equally,
Whether they are old or young, black or white, poor or rich,
I have a dream that I could spread invisible wings
And soar up above the clouds with just one happy thought,
I have a dream that I could invent the elixir of life,
I have a dream that I could be an actress and a singer
And a professional footballer,
I have a dream that I could stop animal testing
And factory farming.

Maddy Vogler (12)
Reepham High School, Norwich

I Have A Dream

Not just a dream,
What are dreams?

I dream of riding a humming bumblebee
And it's taking me across lands,
Lands of sand,
Seas of green,
Things I've never seen,
Pink kangaroos bounding in my fridge,
Where the snow is warm to the touch,
A colossal blue bottle whale,
Diving into the candyfloss clouds,
Sweeping along us and winking,
Where the stars were twinkling.
I flew,
Higher, higher and higher,
Into the shooting star sky,
Where a koala was having a tea party,
On the moon,
It glowed a fantastic fuchsia,
Lighting the way,
To the celebrations,
I was reaching out,
Closing in on this giant crystal ball,
Almost . . .

But suddenly no light,
No koala tea parties,
No shooting star sky,
No blue bottle whale,
Pink kangaroo,
Seas of green, land of sands,
Or humming bumblebee,
I fall,

Plummeting into known boundaries,
Tumbling and turning, I swirl and whirl,
Coming into contact with a grey scorched atmosphere,
I smack my head on something hard,
My floor.

That's what dreams are made of.

Emma Godwin (13)
Reepham High School, Norwich

I Wish

I wish
The world was perfect,
I wish
There was no violence,
I wish
The world was peaceful,
I wish.

I wish for a world,
Where violence was an uncreated crime,
Where global warming and pollution
Were not there,
I wish.

I wish for a land,
Where poverty and droughts were absent
And war was banished for all eternity,
I wish.

I wish all the rainforests,
Were still untouched by
Mankind's fingers,
I wish.

I wish the world was peaceful,
I wish the world was fair,
I wish.

Tasha Ferenczy (12)
Reepham High School, Norwich

If I Could I Would . . .

If I could I would stop the planes from hitting the Twin Towers,
Then stop the mosquitoes from spreading malaria
And stop all the killers in the world from murdering,
Then stop the hungry from dying
And stop all the wars that have happened, or will happen.

If I could I would stop homework because it's a waste of time,
Then stop people from smoking,
Stop people from littering,
Then there would be much more fun in the world
And much more interesting villages.

If I could I would stop homework because I get annoyed with it,
Then bring back the people who have, or will die
And food and drink will be much cheaper
And have bigger and better house
And lots of money.

If I could I would close the schools for a year,
Then earn £10,000,000 a day for doing nothing
And stop people dying in the world,
All families are loving and caring,
Then the world would be a better place.

Samuel Whittaker (11)
Reepham High School, Norwich

Dream

I have a dream, a dream of happiness, not of hatred,
A dream where I am adored,
A dream where hate turns to love,
A dream where your worst enemies become your best friends,
I have a dream where everyone is free,
A dream of freedom,
A dream where there is no poverty,
A dream where everyone alike is even,
I have a dream.

Leon Allen (13)
Reepham High School, Norwich

My Perfect World

In my perfect world, poverty was history
And global warming was dead,
High prices were gone,
Plus nobody smoked.

I had a dream that there was no homework,
School holidays were longer,
It was sunny every day
And there were more shops.

I wish that I had a bigger house,
There was no shouting and screaming,
More holidays
And I had more money.

In my imagination people can fly
And the grass is pink,
The sky is orange
And there is a new animal,
With a rabbit's head and a duck's body.

Natasha Wade (11)
Reepham High School, Norwich

I Wish And I Dream

I have not one wish and one dream,
I have many when I think about it . . .

These are impossible but I still have dreams,
Diseases and illnesses being cured,
Natural disasters never happening again.

Everyone can help with these ones;
No more poverty, racism and animal cruelty,
It's not fair.

My absolute wish is that
My family are happy.

Alice Searjeant (12)
Reepham High School, Norwich

What I Want!

I have a wish that one day
Everyone can live in the world together
Or to stop all the things in the world
That takes people's lives.

I have a dream to ban all cars
And go back to horse and carts
Or that everyone has the same amount
Of money so there are no people
Living on the streets.

I have a dream to have a hunky husband
Like Nigel Harman or a medicine to keep me,
My friends and family alive forever
And everyone wears their pyjamas in the daytime,
That's what I want!

Tayla Menear (12)
Reepham High School, Norwich

My Ideal World

My ideal world would to be
That everyone becomes happy,
Please, no illnesses and no poverty
In our world,
There should be no disasters.

I wish that absolutely everything in the
Shops was free to buy.

I have a dream
That there is more sun in Norfolk,
Always and forever,
There should always be
More pocket money
In my world.

Amy Secker (12)
Reepham High School, Norwich

I Believe In Miracles

I believe in miracles, yes I do,
I believe if everyone put their mind to it,
There would be less poverty.

I believe in miracles, yes I do,
I believe if the floor was made of trampolines,
People wouldn't be as obese.

I believe in miracles, yes I do,
I believe that if bullies changed their ways,
Then people that get bullied will lead better lives.

I believe in miracles, yes I do,
I believe in sunshine and warm rain,
To fill the reservoirs.

I believe in miracles, yes I do,
I believe nothing should be dull
And everything was made of chocolate.

Charlie Skinner (11)
Reepham High School, Norwich

I Dream

I dream that I could fly in a spaceship,
Through the planets, through the stars.
I dream . . .

I dream that I could sail on a boat,
Over the waves, over the sea.
I dream . . .

I dream that I am rich and world famous,
Play football, play rugby.
I dream.

Steven Parker (11)
Reepham High School, Norwich

If . . .

If she would smile,
With true joy once more.

And the anonymous would not torment her,

And they both would stop their weeping . . .

If he would return
Once more,
I know,
I would jump with my heart and happiness . . .

If we would all stop and think to ourselves . . .

If people took care of what they say,
If people weren't hurt by what came their way,
The world might be happy,
The world might be glad,

If . . .

Catrin Hamer (12)
Reepham High School, Norwich

I Had A Dream!

I had a dream . . .
A young girl alone and scared,
A shadow, no love or care,
All she wants is a family that cares,
But all she gets is pain and misery,
She cries at night and cries all day,
A shadow lost and never to be found,
A young girl alone and scared.

Toni Hall (13)
Reepham High School, Norwich

My Dreams

I wish we could walk down the street,
Without wondering who we may meet,
Or panicking when to cross the road,
When lorries come past with their heavy load,
When I walk back, I wonder whether I'll ever get home,
Whilst youngsters speed past while on their phones,
Please just listen to my dreams
And put down your guns and killing machines.
Why is the world in such a rush?
Soon the world will be in one big hush,
Not many people will stay alive,
But those lucky few will survive,
Why can't the world just get along,
While they hear my truthful song?

Sián Sands (12)
Reepham High School, Norwich

I Have An Imaginative Dream

I have an imaginative dream . . .
That I could be the world's strongest man,
That I could be the fittest and healthiest man in the world,
That I could be the world's best footballer,
That I could fly,
That I could be the smartest man alive,
That I would be able to make time freeze,
At the click of my fingers,
But you know what would really make all this good?
Is that if nobody in the world cared!

Grant Cattermull (11)
Reepham High School, Norwich

I Have A Dream . . .

I have a dream, a dream of a perfect world,
A world where there is no poverty, no greed,
No racism and no prejudice,
A world where everyone, no matter their age, race or religion
Can live in harmony,
A world where everyone can use the Earth's resources,
Fairly and equally,
A world where renewable sources of energy are constantly used
And people can walk along a street,
Peacefully and fearlessly,
A world where there is a bright and hopeful future for children,
But this is just a dream, exactly as the title says.

The cruel reality is that,
Half of the world is starving to death, whilst the
Other half is obese and greedy,
Always wanting more, even though they
Already have enough,
Racism, ageism, poverty, greed, prejudice
And religion rule the world,
Deciding who does what, and how much they get paid for it,
Thick black smoke billows out of massive chimneys,
Choking everyone surrounding it,
People walk along the street in fear of being
Mugged or attacked brutally,
Children dread the pollution and global warming,
That they will be faced with soon,
Dreams can soon become reality.

Megan Cross-Gower (13)
Reepham High School, Norwich

I Have A Dream

I have a dream that one day soon, there will be peace in this world,
I have a dream that old people will not be scared to go outside,
I have a dream that nobody will live in poverty ever again,
I have a dream that nobody in this world will ever be hungry,
I have a dream that all illnesses will have a cure,
I have a dream that I could fly and have magical powers,
I have a dream that I could be even more clever.

Frankie Fuller (11)
Reepham High School, Norwich

I Have A Dream!

I wish that one day,
All the bad things would just stop
And money would start to grow on trees.

I wish that I could be on holiday every day
And would never have to work or go to school!

I wish I could marry someone rich and famous!

Shelley Cook (11)
Reepham High School, Norwich

I Have A Dream . . .

Running away from my enemies,
Not getting anywhere,
The floor turning into sticky tar,
My feet sinking,
The enemy is getting closer behind me,
There's nowhere to hide or run.

Emma Skidmore (12)
Reepham High School, Norwich

I Have A Dream

I have a dream where demon's die,
Of Match of the Day and Pukka Pies,
I have a dream where dragons are real
And I have pancakes for every meal,
I have a dream of endless glory
And some of them are really gory,
I have a dream where space travel's quick,
With endless ice cream to lick,
I have a dream of love and care,
Where my family are always there,
I have a dream of many sports
And some of them are out of sorts,
Unchangeable and you're asleep,
Some of them would make you weep.

Joshua Kennedy (12)
Reepham High School, Norwich

I Have A Dream

I have a dream,
That one day I will
Have a car,
An Aston Martin V12 Vanquish.

I have a dream,
That one day I will,
Have a job,
To be a car designer.

I have a dream,
That one day I will,
Have a family,
A family full of love.

I have a dream . . .

Jacob Mears (12)
Reepham High School, Norwich

Thinking Big

Verses of my dreams,
Are spread across a page,
They seep out of my diary,
Escaping from their cage.

They float out of my room,
They don't need a key,
People can listen
And people can see.

They drift down my street
And travel through the town,
Passed along by word of mouth,
My dreams are filtered down.

Beamed out by the telly
And in newspapers read,
Look how far my dreams have flown,
Through the world they've spread.

Lily Tozer (12)
Reepham High School, Norwich

I Have A Dream

I have a dream,
That one day,
Everyone will live in peace,
That no one will be left out of games,
Because of their skin colour,
But because of their
Ability of the game.
Everyone should have the same rights,
That's my dream.

Dean Francis (13)
Reepham High School, Norwich

I Have A Dream

I have a dream that
There was no more war,
Better weather,
Less dangerous animals,
No global warming,
No fines
And more water.

I have a dream that
There were more roads,
A better Norwich City football team,
No schools,
Higher paid jobs,
More old people's helpers,
More skate parks.

I have a dream that
I had a better skateboard,
A wall of stylish Samurai swords,
A bigger house,
A bigger and better garden,
New cars,
More money,
Better neighbours.

I have a dream that
I could visit the spiritual world,
Have laser vision,
To be as smart as a computer.

I have a dream . . .
Of all this stuff.

Cameron Clapton (12)
Reepham High School, Norwich

My Dream

I had a dream I was on a journey,
Throughout the sea, I had a great
Life but until it left me,
When I could see . . .

The lightning *flashing*,
The waves *crashing*,
The darkness *falling*
And people *rushing*
Then I had felt . . .

The rain hitting my skin,
The winds pushing me back,
My stomach turning around
And the coldness freezing my blood
And then I heard . . .

The wind *whistling*,
The people *screaming*,
The thunder *smashing*
And then people *shouting*,
'The ship is *sinking!*'
When I awoke I found out it wasn't a dream!

Anna Brown (13)
Riverside Middle School, Bury St Edmunds

Do Dreams Come True?

I have a dream to become famous,
A singing sensation around the world.

I have a dream to grow up into a kind world,
Where there is no war or fighting.

I dream of a world where children are safe,
Where they feel secure wherever they are.

I dream of a world where politicians listen to what the public want.

I have a dream where global warming
Would become a thing of the past.

I have a dream where everybody would recycle
And landfills are given a chance to decompose.

I dream of a world where cruelty to animals would stop
And they would be treated with respect.

I dream of a world where drought and poverty would be cured,
Making the world a better place.

I have a dream where people would pay attention
And stop polluting our precious surroundings.

I have a dream where people would be happy with how they look
And stop relying on plastic surgery.

I dream of a world where people would open their eyes
And look at the health warnings on cigarettes.

I dream of a world where there are no guns or knives
And people can live in a safe environment.

I have a dream to one day travel the world,
Seeing new cultures and different ways of life.

I have a dream where people with different religions
Can be welcome into our country,
As if they are one of us.

I dream of a world where people all over the globe
Can get along, and live happily, with no worries in life.

Ellie Clarke (11)
Riverside Middle School, Bury St Edmunds

My Poem About My Dream

Hooray! I've won the lottery,
So now I can go on a shopping spree
And get what I want,
However, I won't get too greedy,
I will share it with my family, friends and
Give some to charity.

With the money I have won, I will go on holiday,
The charities I shall give some of the money to are
Cancer Research UK, RSPCA and
Great Ormond Street Hospital,
I will give some to my friends and family,
So they can also get what they want.

If people ring me up asking for money,
I will say no
Because if I give them money, then they would think
It is alright to keep ringing back and asking for more money.

Most people when they win the lottery,
They spend it all at once,
But I will try not to do that,
I will try to keep some in my bank accounts!

When I get given the money,
I would feel very shocked, happy and excited,
My friends and family would be happy for me,
But some people would be jealous of me.

I can hear someone calling my name,
It's my mum,
Oh, I was only having a dream!

Karla Abrey (11)
Riverside Middle School, Bury St Edmunds

Life

At first I thought, a poem about our dreams,
Then I thought, what are my dreams?
As now I feel like I don't know,
Everyone has an aspiration in life,
A point on who they are,
Everyone has a meaning in life
And you just have to figure it out,
You were put on this Earth for a reason
And we all are special and unique,
You have to find your way in life,
Like a big maze,
Sometimes you take a wrong turn,
But you still have to keep going
And now I know what my dream is,
To go through life and see the little things,
Don't rush or miss out a detail,
To live a full life.

Ashley Hegan (11)
Riverside Middle School, Bury St Edmunds

Dreaming

I have a dream
That when I grow up,
I will change the world
And make it a better place.
That I will stop racism altogether
And that I will be a better person,
I have a dream, that I will
Become a police officer
And do the right thing,
That I will be a nurse,
That cares for those who need caring for
And that I will travel the world
And experience the things others may not.
My dream is that others will try and do the same!

Natalie Beckwith (12)
Riverside Middle School, Bury St Edmunds

I Have A Dream

I have a dream
To one day own a pink sports car,
To drive down Oxford Street and go on a shopping spree.

I have a dream
To create a business of my own,
Selling designer fashions and accessories.

I have a dream
To one day get married and have
My honeymoon in the Maldives,
To sit on the beach in the sunshine
And every now and again go in for a paddle,
In the clear blue sea.

I have a dream
To own a luxurious apartment in Florida,
Overlooking the Disney theme park.

Charmaine Harris-Harvey (12)
Riverside Middle School, Bury St Edmunds

I Have A Dream

I have a dream that I'm an Olympic champion at high jumping
And I would punch my fists in the air, the audience
                              would cheer for me,

I have a dream that racism would stop all around the world
And people would treat others as equals.

I dreamt a dream when everyone would take action
To help stop global warming.

I dreamt a dream that I would be rich and famous,
For being a great actress.

I have a dream that people would take care of the environment.
I dreamt a dream that when I die,
I will float up to Heaven and so would all
My friends and family.

Sally Fung (12)
Riverside Middle School, Bury St Edmunds

I Have A Dream

I have a dream that the world would be cooperative,
Not country against country,
There should be peace for everyone,
A country does not make itself better by defeating others,
It makes a country more shameful.

I have a dream there is no racism in the world,
Just because people are different colours
It doesn't make them different, the inside counts,
Racism is despicable.

I have a dream that animals are not hurt by humans,
We should replace meat with another substance,
We wouldn't like it if animals ate us all of the time.

I have a dream that we should explore further into space
And our world, and that we will come across discoveries
That have never been seen before,
They should inform civilians of what they have found,
Not cover up the secrets,
Unlocking never known information.

Tom Gillingham (12)
Riverside Middle School, Bury St Edmunds

I Have A Dream

I have a dream,
That I will play for Chelsea
And win the Premiership,
I have a dream,
That I will score
And win against Arsenal,
I have a dream,
That I will be a superstar
And be known all around
The world as 'The best'.
I have a dream,
That I will play for England,
Wear number 8
And win the World Cup!
I have a dream,
That I will play football
Against professionals
And score the winning
Goal!

Ryan White (12)
Riverside Middle School, Bury St Edmunds

My Dreams For The Future

I have a dream that one day
There will be no more poverty so little children
Don't have to work at the age of five
And they all have a suitable house
For them and their families.

I have a dream that I will be the most skilful
Player Arsenal has ever had,
Even better than Thierry Henry,
The best player in the world!

I have a dream that when I'm older,
I will have a great job and earn good money,
Therefore, I will have a wonderful house
And a Mercedes SLR (Convertible)

I have a dream that I will visit my great grandad
Who lives in the gorgeous place of Brisbane, Australia,
Which I have never been to in my life.

I have a dream there will be no more extinct
Species of animals and that they will ban animal hunting.

I have a dream that the world would be free of diseases,
Famine and doctors will find a cure for cancer.

I have a dream that there will be no more crime,
That people would feel safe in their homes
And wouldn't have to worry about going out alone.

Ryan Nutter (11)
Riverside Middle School, Bury St Edmunds

Paradise Island

My dream is of a paradise island,
Sun, sea and sand,
Crystal clear water and golden beaches,
Sandcastles and sunbathing,
My dream is of swimming and paragliding,
Relaxing and forgetting my worries,
My dream is of a great holiday filled with
Jet skies and snorkelling,
My dream is of a massive adventure,
Exactly how I desire it to be,
My dream is exciting because you never
Know what will happen next,
My dream is like another world, life and time,
My dream is so perfect in every way
And I wouldn't want to change it,
My dream is my own and cannot be copied,
No one can ever have my dream
Because it is so genuine,
Sometimes I wish my dream will never end,
It seems so real until you wake up,
It feels like you're there living it up,
It is a relaxing break full of fun,
My dream is an exciting one.

Danielle Taylor (11)
Riverside Middle School, Bury St Edmunds

Dreams Can Become Reality . . .

I have a dream to one day be,
A famous singer for everyone to know,
I have a dream to help other people
And help them day by day,
I have a dream to go on a peaceful
Holiday on the beach in the great Miami.

In the future, I have a dream that
There will be no wars,
That animals won't be killed just for sports,
I have a dream I could read people's thoughts.

I have a dream that I wouldn't argue with my brother,
That people would be friends and not argue with each other,
I have a dream that the homeless could be given another chance.

I have a dream that everyone will decide about school,
That I could jump from the highest board in the swimming pool,
But not everyone would break the rules.

But my main dream is that our world can be a calm and peaceful place,
For everyone to enjoy!

Millie Royal (12)
Riverside Middle School, Bury St Edmunds

I Have A Dream

I have a dream, in fact I have lots of dreams,
I dream to be rich so I could buy whatever I want,
A Labrador puppy would be what I wished for
As well as having a car so I can ride on the road,
To get no homework, so I won't have to do it,
Maybe to be on TV, to be famous and
Everyone to know and like me,
I have a dream to rule the world
Or become the Queen of England,
I could have everything *my* way,
I could own theme parks in my back garden,
To make a famous film or write a famous novel,
I have a dream that people I absolutely love will never die,
I hope no one will ever rob my home,
Bad people will never exist,
My dream is to live in a luxurious house with my best friends,
I wish there are no more wars or fights,
I could be good at everything I wanted to be,
I dream that the world will be a better place to live in,
But my biggest dream ever is
That all my dreams came true!

Emily Carter (12)
Riverside Middle School, Bury St Edmunds

Explain, Explain

Explain how I can put this into words,
I want to describe to you how the world really works,
We are selfish, greedy and do not share,
People die because we do not care.

We are strangers in this empty space,
We throw things out and use no waste,
Starving children across the world,
Are dying slowly like a flower unfurled.

Natural disasters sweep across the land,
Buildings are destroyed, people can hardly stand,
Take one minute of your life to understand,
How the poor people are living, it was not planned.

Help and show them you care,
By giving your love and all you can spare,
Let's all pull together for the rest of the land
And show the world that *you* understand.

Katelina Fusco (14)
St Andrew's School, Bedford

My Mum

My mum is so kind,
She's always in my mind,
My mum, she's all I see,
Even when I go out to sea.

I love her more than ever,
Mostly in bad weather,
Each drop of rain is like a tear of joy,
She's showing how proud she is of her girl and boy.

Me and my brother
Aren't as happy as we seem,
Because we're only with our mum,
When she's in our dreams.

Victoria Elms (13)
St Andrew's School, Bedford

The Way I Feel For You

He makes all my dreams come true,
My love I owe this all to you,
Please don't let this dream end
Or I won't be able to ever mend!

He's my one and only decent prize,
If he goes away how will I ever survive?
He's the one that I adore,
I couldn't ask for anything more.

I hope he stays forever and a day,
So I can show how much he means to me,
He brightens up my day, if it's ever grey,
No words could ever say how I feel for him,
I really hope he feels this too.

You could put all the love songs in the world together
And they still wouldn't show how much I care for you.

Sarah Eve (14)
St Andrew's School, Bedford

When I Go To Bed At Night . . .

When I go to bed at night,
I close my eyes and shut them tight,
I dream to be an ice skater,
But my brother dreams to be a car racer,
I'll slide and ride down the ice,
But trip over my skates, and fall down twice,
I'll win medals and trophies of gold
And enter competitions of countries untold,
My costume will be sparkly and bright,
So when I slide down the ice, it glows in the icy light,
When I have finished, people will cheer and clap,
As I do my final lap,
Have I won gold? I'll wait and see,
But I know this dream's just a fantasy.

Louise Brentnall (15)
St Andrew's School, Bedford

Can I Fly To The Sky?

My dream is to fly,
Fly to the sky,
Meet all my grandmas and grandads,
I know it sounds mad,
But that's my dream,
To fly.

I can't help but sigh,
All I want to do is fly,
Maybe not to Heaven,
But at least to cloud 11.

Fly to every mountaintop,
To keep on going and not to stop,
Toboggan on the clouds,
To sing, dance and be loud.

My dream is a happy dream,
Although to some people, sad it may seem.

Oh I do wish this could be,
This wonderful flight would just be me,
It would be on a first class seat,
I would be friends with everyone I meet.

This dream doesn't occur when I am asleep,
Or where secrets keep,
No, it actually occurs when I am about to get on a plane,
Maybe it's to Spain.

Oh, this dream definitely will not come true,
Especially when I am waiting in the departure lounge,
For a plane that is overdue!

Eleanor Roblett (12)
St Andrew's School, Bedford

My Medical Dream

My dream is to be a paramedic
And help people on their way,
I would drive to wherever they are,
Or even where they lay,
Looking all around,
I hear a sound,
I've got to set them free,
People crashed in cars,
In a ditch,
I try to get everyone,
Without a single hitch!

I give the people that I find,
First aid treatment straight away,
I try to be kind
And look at what is hurt,
I try to get the patient to listen to me,
To try and stay calm,
Then they should feel a little bit better,
I start the blue flashing alarm,
I need to get to hospital fast,
Helping the patient on the way,
Through the traffic lights I pass.

I zoom along the roads,
Overtaking,
Arriving at the hospital,
I see the doctors race, move out of the way,
Because I'm the best
And I saved the day!

Laura Batchelor (11)
St Andrew's School, Bedford

I Had A Dream . . .

I had a dream that I ruled my house,
I'd kick and scream if I didn't get a mouse,
I'd tell my mum to clean my room
And get my dad to fetch the broom.

I had a dream that I ruled my town,
I'd always wear my great big crown,
I'd get loads of money to buy lots of tops
And if I didn't I'd throw some strops.

I had a dream that I ruled the UK,
I'd make sure everyone was OK,
I'd always listen to some wicked music,
Including my favourite song, 'Just Lose It'.

I had a dream that I ruled all of Asia,
I'd own the tiny country of Malaysia,
I'd meet the short and thin population,
But still I want to own the nation.

I had a dream that I ruled the world,
I'd change my hair, so it wasn't curled,
I'd order a tub of ice cream
And punish people who are mean.

I had a dream that I ruled the Earth,
I'd encourage people to give birth,
I'd help the people who are very poor,
Then I'd welcome them through my door.

I had a dream and it has just left,
It kind of feels like there's been a theft,
I'm glad it disappeared out of my sight,
As now I can see the bright sunlight!

Kimberley Ambrose (11) & Charlotte Northwood (12)
St Andrew's School, Bedford

My Dream

Dreams are funny things,
When you are younger, you dream of having that
Special toy, that dances and sings.

My dreams, I am sad to say,
Were not at all in this way.

I dreamt of being left alone by the bully,
As he would manipulate me carefully.

Saying everything was my fault and bossing me around
And then when things went wrong, he would beat me to the ground,
Until I was black and blue, and made no sound.

I hated going home, as I wasn't loved,
I wished that someone would look down from above,
And say to me,
'Everything will be alright you'll see,
I, God will bring you a loving family.'

Wow! A family! What a dream!
That's a lot better than a toffee ice cream!

I wished these girls at school would stop picking on me,
As I was different from the rest,
I don't care what they think - I'm the best.

I had to kid myself with these dreams,
So that everything seems to be just fine
And a loving and caring family will be just mine!

Kelly Alston (15)
St Andrew's School, Bedford

The Day The Animals Spoke To Me

I had a dream that animals could talk,
Whilst I was going for a walk,
I met a great big ugly toad
And he said, 'Hey, get off the road.'

I walked along a little more,
Then I met a wild boar,
My shirt he took and he tore!
That horrible little wild boar.

I thought about a friend in the past,
A hamster, he was cuddly and fast,
He told me he liked my *Honeynut Loops,*
When he had a bowl, he could jump through the hoops.

My rabbit was different, calm and slow,
It took a while for the words to show,
'Give me lettuce, small and neat,
But whatever you do, don't give me meat.'

Animals, animals everywhere,
They can talk and we must care,
Listen carefully to every sound,
That's what makes the world go around.

Hannah Lewis & Zoe Blair (11)
St Andrew's School, Bedford

I Have Dreams

I have dreams,
The greatest ones yet,
My cat and I will live forever
And we will always be together.

I have dreams,
The greatest ones yet,
I could *zoom* very soon,
To the outer space moon.

I have dreams,
The greatest ones yet,
I would be very calming,
If I could find my handsome Prince Charming.

I have dreams,
The greatest ones yet,
From my heart will come
Always laughter and fun.

I have dreams,
The greatest ones yet,
I could have my own expensive car,
Right now, you can't see me!
As I have driven so far.

I have dreams,
The greatest ones yet,
I shouldn't tell anyone
I want to be rich
Because all they would want to do is snitch.

A dream is a wish your heart makes,
Only I can make these dreams come true,
But you never know, it could be you!

Verity Esaw (13)
St Andrew's School, Bedford

I Dream Of Happiness

I dream of happiness,
The warm contentment of sunshine,
The clouds floating by in the delightful blue sky,
The delicate dewdrops balancing on blades of green grass,
The tightly closed buds, slowly opening to reveal vibrant flowers,
The bright pink water lilies flowing gently downstream,
The young children playing cheerfully in the soft,
                                    fresh fallen blossom,
The families smiling and having fun together,
The waves lapping over the rocks on the beach,
The soft, warm sand on your feet.

Claire Bushell (14)
St Andrew's School, Bedford

As If

I dreamt that I was pretty,
At the moment I get no pity,
I feel I'm on a cloud, but
I'm just stuck in a crowd.
People make fun of me,
They never come round for tea,
I am never glad,
I am always sad,
I sit on my own,
Talking to myself on the phone,
Oh! I am all alone,
I dreamt I was as pretty as Britney Spears,
Oh! I dreamt, I dreamt I was beautiful,
But that will never happen to me, as I am invisible,
If this dream comes true,
It will come out of the blue,
I am glad it is a dream,
For I am who I am.

Caroline Watson (11)
St Andrew's School, Bedford

I Had A Dream

I dreamt I saw a pig that could fly,
I shouted, 'Oh my, oh my!'
He fell to the ground,
With a thud and a pound
And then I began to cry.

I dreamt I saw a floating ghost,
Which at first, I thought was eating toast,
I said, 'Hello,'
But he said 'No!'
And floated off to the coast.

I dreamt I saw a bumblebee,
It winked and grinned and smiled at me,
He flew up high into the sky
And banged into a tree.

And now my dream will have to end,
But I'm sure my head will truly mend!

Deanna Winn (12)
St Andrew's School, Bedford

I Have A Dream

We miss you Grandpa,
Your smile, your love,
We look up to the stars above,
The fun we had, the times in Spain,
I dreamt that you were here again.

Our mum and dad, they hurt so much,
Your helping hand, your loving touch,
We raise a glass and think of you
And know that you can see us too,
I will never forget you.

We'll always dream of you Grandpa.

Emma Hind (12)
St Andrew's School, Bedford

Chocolate Dreams

Chocolate is my pleasure,
My one and only treasure,
Mars, Milky Way and Galaxy,
Everywhere in the universe.

Snickers, Yorkie and Dairy Milk,
Melting in my mouth just like silk,
A block of soft gold melting on my tongue,
My one and only favourite one.

Monday, Tuesday, every day of the week,
The golden colour, caramel and fudge,
My chocolate that's hidden in the secret chocolate box,
The box that my mum would not let me touch.

Chocolate is the best gift,
On Valentine's Day, Christmas and birthdays,
Chocolate is my desire,
Melting like burning hot fire.

Smarties, KitKat, Snickers bar,
A big box of Milky Stars,
Each chocolate has a top, middle and centre,
The more fantastic variety the better.

Chocolate is my pleasure,
My one and only treasure,
Mars, Milky Way and Galaxy,
Everywhere that I want to be,
That's why my dream is to see,
The one and only chocolate factory.

Sejal Chandarana (12)
St Andrew's School, Bedford

I Had A Dream

When I was young,
I was really quite dumb,
I had a dream that
I ate a chocolate seam.

I made a rhyme,
But not a crime,
This dream, it goes like this,

Chocolate is my pleasure,
My one and only treasure,
Galaxy melting on my tongue,
My gorgeous . . . my favourite one.

Smarties, KitKat, Snickers bar,
Buttons, Mars and Milky Way Stars,
Dairy Milk, Crunchie too,
Very special for me and you.

But now my dream,
Comes to an end,
I'm sure my tummy,
Will be kissed better by my mummy!

Emily Hillier (12)
St Andrew's School, Bedford

I Have A Dream - My Granddad

I have a dream . . .
That my granddad would still be alive,
If it's not too much to ask,
As this will be my greatest task,
My granddad was strong, like a ship
And had the most powerful willpower,
We appreciated his love and kindness,
He is in Heaven now and in peace,
He's calm and relaxed,
All our family would love to have him back,
In this discriminatory world,
But it won't come true as we're all drowned
In our sorrow, at your dismissal,
We know how much you appreciated your beer,
As you were never in fear,
You were all so clear,
So friends and family come and pray,
As we want you to come and stay,
As we lay lying, day by day,
You always brought a ray of sunshine,
You were all so fine
And you loved to dine,
We come upon you now, we miss you so much,
So listen up now if you're listening,
As we have something to say,
Goodbye, we all love and miss you, day after day.

Sophie Richardson (13)
St Andrew's School, Bedford

I Have A Dream

If I was to have a dream come true,
It would be for him to come back,
We would go for a picnic and have a snack,
If I was to have a dream come true,
He would be there when I come home,
Instead of me, my mum and sister being alone.
If I was to have a dream come true,
He would be there to help me with my homework,
Instead of driving me berserk,
If I was to have a dream come true,
He wouldn't have left us for her
And he would just magically appear,
If I was to have a dream come true,
He would be with me and my sister,
And my mum, he would love her.
I stopped believing in kings and princes with their swords,
I stopped believing in my family being famous,
My mum, a lady, my dad, a lord,
I stopped believing in the tooth fairy
And elves and little things,
I stopped believing in miracles and angels with their wings,
I stopped waiting for my fairy tale,
As I knew it would never come true,
But I'm still waiting, waiting for you,
Even though I know you won't come,
I stopped believing in Santa Claus
And things I never had,
But the thing I never stopped believing is,
That you will always be my dad.

Gabriella Farrow (12)
St Andrew's School, Bedford

I Have A Dream

A dream is sweet,
A dream is a sound,
It works in this big fluffy cloud,
I have a dream,
It's like a wish,
I wish when I'm older,
I'll have lots of horses
And to top it all off, to live
In this really big mansion, with lots of stables,
As well as working with the horses,
I will walk down the street,
In my best fashionable clothes,
Diamond rings with lots of fabulous jewellery,
That will make me look so bling,
So a dream is sweet,
A dream is sound,
But the best dream of all,
Works in the world's best fluffy cloud.

Nicola Brentnall (13)
St Andrew's School, Bedford

I Have A Dream

I have a dream that I have the most beautiful looks,
I have a dream that I have light brown locks,
I have a dream that I have sapphire eyes,
I have a dream that I would never have to try,
I have a dream that heads would turn,
Just to get a look at me,
I have a dream that I have a golden key,
I have a dream I do what I can,
I have a dream that I'm happy as I am.

Charlotte Walker (12)
St Andrew's School, Bedford

I Have A Dream

I have a dream to design a dress and
Make it the best for the bride to wear,
I dare to make it on my own,
What will happen?
I don't know.

The dress will be white and quite a sight,
It might even give people quite a fright.

Frills and ruffles in the air,
A sight not many can compare,
It frightens the birds up in the trees
And farmer Giles said,
'I'll have one please!'

Lucy Darnell (14)
St Andrew's School, Bedford

My One Dream

Every day I feel you near me,
It makes me happy,
If you're around me, you comfort me,
Save me from evil
And help me with the life that I have
Not seen before,
I'd love to be in the sky with you,
We could dance in the clouds
And I could have *big hugs*,
I would be happy forever,
If I was with you,
My grandad.

Fraya Brinkman (11)
St Andrew's School, Bedford

If I Had A Dream

If I was to have one dream . . .

It would be to have lots of money,
Not my mum or my dad, but me!
I would spread my money everywhere,
I would only give out money if I dare,
I would spend my money on loads of designer things!

Bags, dresses, shoes and rings,
Gucci, Armani, Prada too,
All the best for me and you,
Louis Vuitton has the best things,
If I had this stuff, I would probably be friends with kings.

Diesel, D&G, Burberry too,
Loads more also for me and you,
So many things
And quite a lot of bling,
So much bling to cover your ring.

Big house,
With no mouse in it,
To come home every day,
Looking at the things you buy every May,
Gold and silver,
Diamonds and rubies,
All sorts of things for me.

I wish I had lots of money!

Holly Wheldon
St Andrew's School, Bedford

Being Bullied!

I wake one Monday morning,
Dreading the school day once again,
I get changed into my *too large* school uniform,
Only to accept that I will be laughed at, once again,
I pack my bag ready for school,
Finding my homework to be in shreds, once again,
I leave the house, closing the door behind me,
Relieving myself from home stress, once again,
I walk down the path, conscious of the neighbours staring,
I feel worthless and small, once again,
After a long day, it's the end of school,
Nothing's happened, that's unusual,
I dart out of school the back way,
To find them waiting for me.
I wake up on the pavement, bleeding and bruised,
Hoping it's all a dream,
It isn't.

You may feel alone,
But it isn't only you who is being bullied,
Eight out of ten children have been bullied,
Share your problems with others,
Before it gets as bad as this
And then your dream just might come true.

Rebecca Brinkley (13)
St Andrew's School, Bedford

Make The World Smile

Forced smiles on all who feel the pain,
Suffering in silence, again and again,
Every day, new scars appear on the skin,
Some on the outside, some deep within.

The poorest children, frail and weak,
A decent meal is all they seek,
Many losing parents to poverty or disease,
Somebody help them, somebody please!

Old ladies afraid to go out of the door,
With the fear of muggings, raping or more,
Terrified whenever a stranger is near,
It must be terrible, living in fear.

Children and adults in hospital wards,
Waiting for cures, lonely and bored,
With so many illnesses it's hard to survive,
You should be glad that you're still alive.

When I grow older, my wish is to see,
This world and its people all trying to be,
Much better to each other, loving and kind
And make a great future, for all of mankind.

My dream is simple and very clear,
Let the world see and let the world hear,
It's time to put an end to all this
And live in happiness, love and bliss.

So next time someone around you is down,
Give them a smile and get rid of their frown!
And if this spreads, the world will soon be
A much better place for you and for me.

Holly Holt (13)
St Andrew's School, Bedford

With Just One Hand

I had a dream that global warming would stop
And the North and South Pole would stop getting hot,
I dreamt I could stop it with one hand
And stop the sun from burning the land,
I dreamt I could stop racism with just two words,
And world peace would start,
I dreamt I could stop the world from falling apart.

Caroline Watson (12)
St Andrew's School, Bedford

Grandad

A dream I had, he'd be here with me,
He'd come from above,
Floating like a dove,
A dream I had, he'd be here with me,
We'd be together,
Forever and ever,
A dream I had, he'd be here with me,
He'd hold me tight,
If someone tried to get me, he'd put up a fight,
A dream I had, he'd be here with me,
He was so generous and nice,
He gave life a spice,
A dream I had, he'd be here with me,
If I had a choice,
I'd love to hear his voice,
I dream I had, he'd be here with me,
I wish I could meet him again for one last time,
To say how much I love him and that he is mine,
But you could make my dream come true,
If you do, I owe it to you.

Amandeep Rai (12)
St Andrew's School, Bedford

I Had A Dream

I had a dream that I had friends!
It was a lovely dream full of
Butterflies and kindness and
Love for each other,
I had a dream that everyone
Liked me, and that I wasn't
Rejected for who I am,
I had a dream that my family
Was still together and that
We lived in a beautiful home,
With a garden!
I had a dream that my mum
Had stopped drinking and
That my dad was out of prison,
I had a dream that my sister
Was still alive,
But, it was just a dream.

Carrie-Ann Minty (13)
St Andrew's School, Bedford

In The Same Boat

Rest In Peace my gravestone said,
But you will all act as if you're glad I'm dead.

Wastelands, deserts, dried up creeks,
Polluted seas, starving people, iceless peaks.

Littered streets, new diseases, animals leaving,
Ozone's gone, all depleted - toxic breathing.

GM crops are all about big and shiny but with no taste,
Fishes swim through human waste,
Tall chimneys belch out toxic crap,
Covering cities, towns and maps.

So *Rest in Peace* my gravestone said,
I am the Earth and the Earth is dead.

Katie Garner (13)
Sandye Place School, Sandy

I Have A Dream

I have a dream that racism is tackled
And no grandchild will hear of the name.

Imagine all the people that have cancer just get a yellow,
So now they won't die, think of all the lives that could be saved.

I have a dream that someone cures poverty by saving a penalty
And then we have a keeper who can save all penalties.

Imagine the world without medicine, then there
Will be too many free kicks,
Then there would be loads of bookings and
People will get the red card.

I have a dream that there is grass all over Africa
And then there would be food for the cows and for the players.

Imagine no hijackers in the world today,
Then people wouldn't need to go to court or prison.

I have a dream that when Stevie G takes a corner,
A terrorist gets what he deserves.

Imagine all the people, that if this comes true
And how they will live differently.

I have a dream and that dream is,
To make all that I've said come true.

Chris Gregory (13)
Sandye Place School, Sandy

Problems

All over the world, there is something to change,
But the problems are in a gigantic range,
They go from being in our own town,
To all over the world, in many a place.

Locally there are things like graffiti and violence,
These problems cannot be solved by money - hence
The fact that the problems remain, as everyone
Has not quite discovered that problems can be
                      solved without money.

In my country, England of Europe,
For these problems there is hope,
Because our country is populated and powerful,
We can bond together to give ourselves a chance.

There is racism and crime,
Which we're stamping out, as it is a prime target,
It proves our future can be changed,
If the stronger countries use their attributes well.

There are problems - little and small in our country,
Every one of the problems is being drained at a need,
So our country can become a great nation
And set a fine example for other countries to follow.

There are greater problems overseas,
Which are killing millions, take for example, poverty,
It is decreasing in the world, but I feel
It is not decreasing quickly enough.

But all problems are being defeated,
Whether on our first attempt to solve or a repeat attempt,
Let countries link together in arms,
To become one massive continent.

I come to the end of my poem,
Deceive the problems of the world,
They are puzzles waiting to be solved.

Jack Tortoise (12)
Sandye Place School, Sandy

A World Without . . .

A world without drugs,
The suffering of those who lie and steal,
To achieve their fix,
The suffering of those who watch them,
Wither and die,
With feelings so mixed.

A world without wars,
Those that wage anger and hate,
In the name of God,
Prepared to take a life,
Or bring a country to its knees,
With nothing more than a wink or a nod.

A world without cruelty to animals,
The fox running for his life,
Until caught and tortured, the pain, the hurt,
The proud elephant brought down to die for his tusks,
Such beautiful creatures,
Why do we treat them like dirt?

A world without poverty,
The starving millions without food or hope,
Filling our television screens as we sit down to eat,
Their sad eyes pleading,
Arms outstretched
And we turn away, unmoved and throw the dog a treat.

A world without discrimination,
Black and white working together,
Without prejudice or mistrust,
The rich concerned for the poor
And the able-bodied lending a willing hand,
Isn't this what we were created for?

Adam McGrath (12)
Sandye Place School, Sandy

I Have A Dream

Sitting on the park bench,
Watching the day go by,
Watching the world change,
Right before our eyes.

Look at the world
And the people around,
Graffittied walls
And the littered ground.

Watching the news,
World leaders sit back,
'Don't worry,' they say,
'Here's an information pack.'

Look up at the sky,
Grey and gloomy,
Gas pollution,
Petrol is fuming.

Watching outside a window,
A war with people in pain,
Running away from the torture,
Wishing they were all sane.

Looking at different countries,
People alone and cold,
The famine and poverty,
Their families being sold.

Sharnie Partridge (12)
Sandye Place School, Sandy

Together As One!

Pollution, war, global warming too,
I have a dream, what about you?

AIDS, death, anguish and fear,
Children and adults alike, shed a tear.

My dream is for all of this to stop,
Farmers alone growing their crops.

Fewer cars will be driven, also less war,
That's what we are on the planet for.

Stand up for others, that's what I believe,
Face up to the truth, stop being naïve.

We are the future, it's up to us to fight,
For what we believe in, with all of our might.

We are united, together as one,
We have to undo all of what has been done.

Obstacles will obscure our path,
Towards justice and peace all over the Earth.

We need to look forward and keep striding on,
If we don't, the world as we know it will be gone.

So now I go, listen to what I say,
You cannot ignore that we are killing the world today!

Jordan Leigh (13)
Sandye Place School, Sandy

Friends

Friends for now, a friend forever laughs for now but not forever.

I remember when we were four, it was our first birthday party,
Our mums bought us new dresses for the occasion,
Yours was yellow and mine was purple,
At the end of the day they were covered in food, dust, mud and
Anything else we could find. Those were the good days.

Friends for now, a friend forever laughs for now but not forever.

I remember when we were seven, you came round mine for the day,
Were supposed to paint on paper but ended up painting
On ourselves, those were the good days.

Friends for now, a friend forever laughs for now but not forever.

I remember when we were ten, you said something to me
Which I never thought I would hear. You said I was your best friend
Ever, and I said the same, those were the good days.

This was the worst day ever, I remember this like the back of my hand,
you said to me that you were moving away and would never
Return . . .
I started to laugh, I thought you were joking, 'Good trick,' I said,
But it wasn't a joke at all. After all that we had been through.

Friends for now, a friend forever laughs for now but not forever.

I lost touch from you for four years . . .
But when I was writing this poem you rang me,
You called me after all this time,
Now we are all grown up, not those silly little girls we once were,
We still have got all those memories about when we were little,
But ready to start new ones.

Friends for now, a friend forever laughs for now but not forever.

Carla Dring (12)
Sandye Place School, Sandy

Imagine All The People

Imagine all the people,
Including blacks and whites,
From all different faiths,
Living in a world of peace.

Where racism is never a part of people's minds,
Where poverty is not an option at all,
Where people walk equal and tall
And terrorism does not threaten mankind.

A world where our leaders,
Put people first and heed us,
Where medicine's within the reach,
Of rich and poor, equal between us.

Imagine where children learn and play,
Without fear brought to each new day,
Where they laugh and sleep free,
From hunger, slavery and poverty.

A world where peace in every country is unlocked,
Where hands united and help is never blocked,
By selfish rulers and greedy men,
Who stop at nothing in their plots.

Is this just a dream,
From a boy's naïve mind,
Or could we make it real
And serve all mankind?

Imagine all the people,
Including blacks and whites,
From all different faiths,
Living in a world of peace.

Joseph Olaniran (12)
Sandye Place School, Sandy

I Have A Dream

Think of a world,
That did not have war as a word,
Guns that were weaker than voices,
Mines that were nothing compared to human peace,
That is my dream.

Think of a world,
Where today's terrorists are tomorrow's helpers,
Where the Twin Towers existed and people had happy families,
There was no London bombings - just a sharing London,
That is my dream.

Think of a world,
Where the sweltering country of Africa,
Had clean water and waterproof houses,
That poor people found jobs,
And had smiles on their faces,
That is my dream.

Think of a world,
Where bullies were weak
And they could not use their fists,
They became policemen and helped others,
That is my dream.

Think of a world,
Where racist people are gone
And everyone respected everyone,
No one hated no one,
That is my dream.

Think of a world,
Where no one drove cars
And there was a clean world,
That is my dream,
I don't want it to be a dream,
I want it to be real.

Tom Hull (11)
Sandye Place School, Sandy

I Have A Dream

I have a dream,
That people of different races,
Although strange they seem,
Will be equal - not judged by faces.

I have a dream,
That there will be no hurt or war,
People will care for others,
Homeless or poor.

I have a dream,
That banished all drugs,
People are not beaten,
No rapists, nor thugs.

I have a dream,
That all people are healthy,
Asian, Jamaican,
Poor or wealthy.

I have a dream,
That there is no global warming,
All the right weather,
Not too sunny, not always cooling.

I have a dream,
That there is no pollution,
No animals at death's edge,
But it all seems a devolution of life.

I have a dream,
That hate didn't exist,
Every face was beaming,
All was equal, loved and kissed.

I have a wish!
I wish that all the dreams that
I have would only come true,
To make the world a better place.

Carly Brinkley (12)
Sandye Place School, Sandy

I Have A Dream, A Dream, My Dream

Remember . . .
A word is more powerful than a gun,
A voice is more powerful than an army.

My dream . . .
Forests of flowers and trees will grow,
No one will feel low,
People will stay calm and won't fight,
Kids could stay out until late at night.

Parent's wouldn't need to worry,
People would stop being in such a hurry,
The streets will be clean,
You wouldn't find things on the floor, like polystyrene.

There's no such thing as war,
No one is poor,
Everyone's treated with respect
And no one will be neglected.

People would care,
Everything was fair,
People were their own,
Without being known.

No one was greedy,
No one was needy,
You did not have to worry about drugs,
Or being scared of thugs.

Imagine people weren't violent
And everyone loved the parliament,
People offered to help out
And there was no such thing as drought.

Imagine dreams came true,
Well they do!

Josie Bullock (11)
Sandye Place School, Sandy

I Have A Dream

I have a dream . . .
That global warming will come to a halt,
For God's sake it's not the world's fault,
I have a dream . . .
That animal cruelty will stop,
Why should they suffer, they suffer a lot,
I have a dream . . .
That racism will stop,
That the people that do it, will just go pop,
I have a dream . . .
That hunting will die,
What harm do animals do, just by walking by?
I have a dream . . .
That bombers will die,
Why should people die, for one stupid lie?

I have a dream . . .
That people won't deal drugs,
Because I think they're all thugs,
I have a dream . . .
That all wars will end,
So we can all come together,
And be friends,
I have a dream . . .
That poverty was gone,
Because I think it's very wrong,
I have a dream . . .
That abuse would end,
Then abused people could make a friend.

Laura Jones (12)
Sandye Place School, Sandy

I Have A Dream

I have a dream where terrorism is stopped
And where we are free to walk down the street
Without being checked for explosives,
Then I see a building collapse.

I have a dream where we are not under rule
By one oppressive ruler and where we have
The freedom of speech,
Then I hear of people being killed
Because of one thing they've said.

I have a dream where we all have enough to eat
And where no one is starving to death,
Then I see pictures of children with their bones
Visible because they are so thin.

I have a dream where we are not scared
About pollution causing global warming,
Then I hear that ice at the Poles is gone forever.

I have a dream where we are all treated equally
And where we are not made fun of because of
Our colour or religion,
Then I see bullies beating up a black Hindu.

I have a dream where there is no obesity and where
We are all healthy and well,
Then I see fat people walking along with a burger
In each hand.

I have a dream where there is enough clean water
For everyone and where everyone has enough to
Drink, then I hear of children dying
After drinking dirty water.

I have a dream where when people ask us,
'Am I safe here?' we can answer with confidence, 'Yes!'
Then I hear of a whole family being murdered by one
Man overnight.

I have a dream were we don't need to be constantly
Checking our wallets and purses to check if they're still there,
Then I hear of someone stealing someone's wallet
Containing £1000!

I have a dream where we have discovered a cure
To many of the diseases that harm the people of the Earth,
Then I hear of innocent people dying of cancer.

I have a dream where everyone plays their part and recycles,
Then I hear of how we are polluting our Earth
By stuffing it full of rubbish.

I have a dream where we all live in peace and harmony
And not under the threat of war,
Then I hear of armed forces marching into an Iraqi town.

I have a dream where we are not always grieving for loved ones,
Unnecessarily,
Then I hear of the many man-made deaths in the world!

I have a dream of a better world and of a better place to live,
I have a dream that at the moment
Is just a dream,
I want my dream to be reality!

Andrew Robinson (11)
Sandye Place School, Sandy

I Have A Dream

I have a dream that there will be peace,
People with smiling faces, at least.

I have a dream that murders will stop,
Or the world will just drop.

And I can't forget racism,
It's a sort of fascism.

If only everyone had a bit of good in them,
Then there wouldn't be any more terrorism.

If people don't keep on dying,
Then there would be less crying.

I'm saying this because I hope it will come true,
If I can say it, so can you.

Lawrence Franklin (13)
Sandye Place School, Sandy

I Have A Dream . . .

I have a dream . . .
That the global warming should come to a stop
And quit with a fling and a hop,
I have a dream . . .
That the world won't deal drugs,
Instead they should give kisses and hugs,
I have a dream . . .
That there was no litter,
Because it makes the world so bitter,
I have a dream . . .
That the world will go on forever,
No more guns, never, no never!
I have a dream . . .
That death will be gone,
So that no one will die and birds
Will always fly,
I have a dream . . .
That there was no poverty,
Because I think life should be a novelty,
I have a dream . . .
To stop animal cruelty
Because it's not fair,
Without animals, the world would be bare,
I have a dream . . .
That there was no bombs,
To make all these dreams come true,
We should all pray and sing songs.

Naomi Morris (12)
Sandye Place School, Sandy

I Have A Dream

Think of a world,
With no wars,
But happiness and peace
And the guns shoot happiness,
That is my dream.

Think of a world,
With no thefts,
But people who gave stuff away
And drug addicts that injected love,
That is my dream.

Think of a world,
With no poverty,
But with love and joy
And the world was polluted with bliss,
That is my dream.

Think of a world,
With no terrorists,
But there were bombs of tranquillity
And cars that could run on love,
That is my dream.

Think of a world,
With no racism,
But where all people are equal
And the bullies beat you with love,
That is my dream.

Arron Davies-Sond (12)
Sandye Place School, Sandy

The Ultimate Showdown Of Ultimate Destiny

The world has changed into a murder scene,
What has happened to the day when we were clean?
Everything has gone from good to bad,
Is this the ultimate showdown of ultimate destiny?

The world has changed into a place where drugs rule people's lives,
What has happened to the day when we were clean?
People needlessly killing and destroying everything,
Is this the ultimate showdown of ultimate destiny?

The world has changed into a place where we speak before thinking,
What has happened to the day when we were clean?
Racism has come back and now more genocide has begun,
Is this the ultimate showdown of ultimate destiny?

The world has changed into a place where you are rich
Because of your strength,
What has happened to the day when we were clean?
If you want money all you have to do is kill, this isn't right,
Is this the ultimate showdown of ultimate destiny?

The world has changed into a place where slaves are
More common than anything,
What has happened to the day when we were clean?
If you want something doing, you just point a gun,
Is this the ultimate showdown of ultimate destiny?

The world has changed into a place where education
Has been abandoned,
What has happened to the day when we were clean?
People just fight for money and to win respect,
Is this the ultimate showdown of ultimate destiny?

Has God forsaken us?
This is no government,
I wish that things never changed,
I think this is the showdown of ultimate destiny.

Brian Andrew (13)
Sandye Place School, Sandy

I Have A Dream

I have a dream to put things right,
Things that are wrong,
The whole of it's a fight,
The world isn't perfect,
With the things that surround it,
Poverty, racism, religion and war,
The whole thing's becoming a bore,
It's going on for so long,
The whole of it's just wrong,
Greet and guilt,
Sparks of selfishness, also hate,
It all started off as a big debate,
None of this is fair,
For people who want to share.

Emotion and pain people go through,
When none of it's their fault,
But what can we do?
We come here to be free,
But look what's happening,
It disgusts me,
Accusations being made,
Lies and hatred are to stay,
I have a dream, that none of this was meant to be,
Instead look at this, we're never going to be free.

Sabina Nessa (13)
Sandye Place School, Sandy

I Have A Dream

I have a dream that the cancer of drugs,
Is dispelled by the medicine of love.

I have a dream that the cyst of terrorism,
Is cut out of the body of society.

I have a dream that the tumour of racism,
Is washed away with a tablet of acceptance.

I have a dream that the deep cut of religion,
Is cleaned by truth and sewn up by time.

I have a dream that the rash of war,
Is wiped away with the cream of peace.

I have a dream that the flu of earthquakes,
Is blown away with the tissue of nature.

I have a dream that the fungus of abortion,
Is sprayed away with love and happiness of motherly union.

Lisa Stevens (13)
Sandye Place School, Sandy

I Have A Dream

Litter, litter everywhere,
Cans, plastic bags and everything messy,
Rape is like a big disaster,
Homeless people crying with starvation,
Fighting is painful, blood splashing,
Everywhere, people dying,
Drugs are stupid, not worth the consequences,
Or side effects.

Now look at these streets, nice and clean,
No wrappers, no bags,
Now there's no rapes, how good is that?
Homeless people have got homes, eating food,
No fighting, so no blood,
No more drugs to ruin people's lives.

Donna West (11)
Sandye Place School, Sandy

I Have A Dream

I have a dream that all the countries
In the world would get on,
So that there would be no war,
Would we be richer if there was no war?

I have a dream that all natural disasters would disappear,
Because all they do is confuse and muddle.

I have a dream that all illnesses and germs
Would not effect the human race.

I have a dream that the terrorists that bomb planes
Will just think about what they are doing
And how many people they are killing, and stop.

I have a dream that the rich and selfish people
Would share it with the people who need it most,
Because if they don't, the really poor people will become
Desperate and start breaking the law.

I have a dream that nobody in the world would
Worry about the colour of other people's skin,
Whether they are white or black,
It doesn't matter what is on the outside,
It's what's on the inside that matters.

Ashley Rees (12)
Sandye Place School, Sandy

I Have A Dream

My dream is that there will be no more terrorism,
No bombs and fire, no madness and crying,
No pressure and guns and no one dying,
No more hearing sirens for miles and miles
And emergency vehicles racing down the road,
People screaming everywhere, people will always
Remember this day forever, by memory of course
And things and people they have lost
And nothing can make up for that.

Shaun Chapman (12)
Sandye Place School, Sandy

I Have A Dream

I have a dream,
A dream about the world,
That we're living in,
A dream to turn things around,
Look out of your window,
Look into your street,
Your town, village, your world,
What do you see?
Strewn rubbish?
Overflowing bins? A gloomy atmosphere?
Air that's polluted? Black smoke?
Unhappy faces?
But who is to blame?
Is it us?
Have you ever stopped,
Before you threw litter,
Before you littered your habitat?
Who is to blame for pollution?
Is it us?
Stop before you open your car.

Have you ever thought it is us that's causing pollution?
So think, think before you act,
Because it is us ruining our world,
Try to stop,
Try to clean your habitat,
Try to bring good thoughts,
Try not to demolish your world,
So, stop the junk,
Stop the garbage,
Stop the trash, the rot, the waste,
Stop it all,
Close your eyes,
Think of a world,
Dream of a world,
What do you see?
Stop dreaming, start acting!

Lola Idris (12)
Sandye Place School, Sandy

I Have A Dream

Some people have a dream to be an actor,
Some people have a dream to be a popstar,
Some people have a dream to be a footballer,
I have a dream for the litter to be put in bins.

Some people have a dream to be a boxer,
Some people have a dream to be a pilot,
Some people have a dream to be a soldier,
I have a dream where there's no poverty.

Some people have a dream to be a doctor,
Some people have a dream to be a vet,
Some people have a dream to be a nurse,
I have a dream where there is no bullying.

Some people have a dream to be a magician,
Some people have a dream to be clever,
Some people have a dream to be pretty,
I have a dream where there's a rule that everyone is equal.

Some people have a dream to have money,
Some people have a dream to feel good,
Some people have a dream to work,
I have a dream where there is no war.

Some people have a dream to be popular,
Some people have a dream not to be bullied,
Some people have a dream to be well known,
I have a dream where there's nothing harmful.

We all have dreams, the idea is to stick with them.

George Hutson (12)
Sandye Place School, Sandy

My Dream

I have a dream that one day,
Everyone will have a full tummy like mine.

A dream that everyone will have a safe home like mine.

A dream that everyone will get a chance to earn money
For themselves and be able to look after their family.

A dream that everyone would get on,
No more violence to each other or themselves.

A dream that people never get diseases and
Lead a good life and be able to see their
Grandchildren grow up.

A dream that everyone would be treated the same
Whatever their religion and stop racism.

My dream ends here, where everyone leads a good life,
That includes my dreams.

Kelly Wall (12)
Sandye Place School, Sandy

I Have A Dream

Racism,
I have a dream that one day,
Every human being will be treated the same,
Equally, no matter what colour they are,
People shouldn't just abuse others because of their skin,
Martin Luther King, what would you do if you watched a
Football match from the sidelines, spoilt by idiots called hooligans?
Would you stand and stare like we have to, or would you
Make a difference?
I think we need more people just like
Martin Luther King,
So save the day and be good and smart.

Daniel Olaniran
Sandye Place School, Sandy

Why?

Why do the wars have to start?
Why does it have to ruin our lives?
Why can't we live in peace,
Not having to think about someone killing us?
Why are there people starving?
Why can't they have some food?
Why do people have to steal?
Why do they have to break the rules?
I want peace and I want to feel like birds flying,
I want to be free to walk and not be scared,
I want people to have food and shelter,
I want people to be happy, and never be sad,
So let's try to stop it forever.

Hanna Chupryna (12)
Sandye Place School, Sandy

The Future

I hope the future is full of robots,
People living on other planets.

Aliens as neighbours, school trips to
Mars, holidays on the moon.

People living underwater,
People living underground,
People living on Pluto,
People living on Jupiter.

Hover cars and hover bikes,
Humungous skyscrapers,
No more war, no more poor,
The future looks good.

Shane Poulter
Sandye Place School, Sandy

Poverty

Asia, Africa, the world's the same,
Poverty happens every day,
Children in every country, wasting away,
Parents dying, children crying.

Babies, children, parents alike,
They're always trying to win a fight,
The parents have died, now the children are new,
They hold on tight and hope for the best.

Food, shelter and medicine is all they need,
Their last resort is to plead,
This may be a nightmare to you,
But it's real for them,
They can't joke about it, or pretend.

If you were there
And saw their faces,
Would you joke and pretend it's all a lie?

To search for food, to be disappointed,
Because there are no resources.

Having nothing in the world to see
Them through the days,
This is why we need to change our ways.

Frances Bell (12)
Sandye Place School, Sandy

I Have A Dream

Doves will fly across the nation,
Bringing peace and happiness,
I have a dream,
Racists will sit down and leave
Their hateful ways,
I have a dream,
Vandals will give up and leave what they have done,
We will forgive,
I have a dream,
Poverty will be of the past
And health and wealth will go
Out to a nation,
I have a dream,
One man will stand up and speak up for peace
And hope it will be heard,
I have a dream,
A saviour, a person will help and love people
For who they are,
He is setting an example, let us follow,
I have a dream,
I had a nightmare of how life is now,
Pollution, murders, terrorists, mammoth crimes
Of hatred and disgust,
We have a dream,
Let's make it reality.

Thomas Hunt (12)
Sandye Place School, Sandy

I Have A Dream

I have a dream that in the future,
Pollution might take over this world,
It might not, it could be pollution free,
I hope that this world isn't polluted.

I have a dream that in the future,
Global warming will not flood this world,
It might not if we stop it,
I hope that this world will not flood.

I have a dream that in the future,
Weapons of mass destruction will not threaten this world,
It might not happen if we don't make them,
I hope that this world will not be destroyed because of them.

I have a dream that in the future,
Racists won't get even worse in this world,
It might not if we stop them,
I hope that this world will stop racism.

I have a dream that in the future,
Darkness in the world will not take over,
It might not if we light this world,
I hope that we will not go into darkness.

I have a dream that in the future,
The seas will not dry up because of the sun spreading,
I hope this will never happen,
Unfortunately this will probably happen.

Joe Keir (12)
Sandye Place School, Sandy

A Dream

Bad issues,
To what would seem,
The land is concrete,
I'm trapped in my dream,
With darkness and sleet.

The sky is black,
There are no people here,
The pollution is back
And so is the fear.

Power is a trance,
But there is one,
There is a chance,
That a single word might stun.

A peaceful dream
The world is good,
The world is clear,
There I stand,
Without a sneer.

The world is saved,
Without a gun,
The power we craved,
For a single word might stun.

The plants grow large,
Up the wall,
Still growing strong
And very tall.

So the concrete was thrown
And the world has been done,
Who would have known,
That a single word could stun.

Peace . . .

Daniel Day (12)
Sandye Place School, Sandy

I Have A Dream

I have a dream that one day,
Nature and the environment will be free,
I have a dream that terrorists will leave
Everything and everyone alone,
I have a dream that one day
People and animals will not be judged
By what they look like,
But by what they do,
I have a dream that pollution will stop,
A dream where there is no violence
Or suicide or even murderers,
A dream for this world to be in peace,
I have a dream that one day
No one is racist or prejudiced,
I have a dream for war to have
Never been invented,
A dream that kids are allowed to
Do anything good they want,
I have a dream that child abusers
Will turn into child lovers.

I have a dream! Do you?

Imogen Partridge (11)
Sandye Place School, Sandy

Nuclear Weapons

Nuclear weapons are too dangerous to be kept,
So get rid of them before it's too late,
They can destroy the Earth,
It will divide the Earth,
Disarm the nuclear bombs,
They will destroy the Earth,
They are mass murderers,
Disarm them before
Doomsday is here.

Michael Bodi (12)
Sandye Place School, Sandy

I Have A Dream

I have a dream,
That pollution will vanish
And all the bad things banished,
To what it would seem.

I have a dream,
That there would be no wastelands
And no one would disband
And everyone would beam.

I have a dream,
That there would be no greediness,
Also there would be no neediness
And that isn't extreme.

I have a dream,
Of a world full of fairness
And not as much carelessness,
A world not making everyone scream.

I have a dream,
For a world without wars
And a world full of open doors,
Do you have a dream?

Arron McLoughlin (12)
Sandye Place School, Sandy

My Dream

I have a dream . . .
That everyone would have a home like me,
A dream that everyone would not starve and be sick,
A dream that everyone would talk to each other,
A dream that everyone can be equal,
A dream that everyone would stop this racism,
A dream that everyone would have a full tummy like mine,
My dream ends here, that everyone lives a life like me,
Be thankful for what you have!

Lauren Keeble (12)
Sandye Place School, Sandy

Easy Sorrow, Dream Of Tomorrow

Dear Hope,
All is black and the door is closed,
The candle is out and it's dark,
The threat of the world is posed,
Have you gone out with the lark?

Dear Hope,
I see you,
Hear you but everything is mute
And I'm blind,
Life is short and I'm left behind,
Are you coming back?

Dear Hope,
Global warming, cold air swarming,
More surges of animals die,
People killing, countries chilling,
Who can change this lie?

Dear Hope,
I am in this dream, it's not any brighter,
To live in this world, my heart has to be a fighter,
I can't change this world alone,
My dream is stuck in a danger zone.

Dear Hope,
I need people on my side,
To help us collide - in darkness,
On flickers the candle, is it too late?
I'm at your coffin handle.

Dear Hope,
I have a dream the world will change,
But only when the last bear dies,
The snow falls when the warm sun shines,
Will we realise that the world needs us
And we need the world!

Danielle Hutchinson (11)
Sandye Place School, Sandy

I Have A Dream

I have a dream that everyone gets along,
That the world is peaceful,
That all quarrels stop,
I have a dream and I am in it.

I have a dream that war will stop,
That everyone is rich,
That nobody is left out,
I have a dream and you are in it.

I have a dream that people are nice,
That children and women are safe,
That everyone is as special as the Queen,
I have a dream and we are in it.

I have a dream that my true love will find me,
That love does not hurt when you break up,
That no one dies through love,
I have a dream and we are in it.

I have a dream that animals are loved,
That animals aren't hunted for fur,
That people aren't cruel to them,
I have a dream and they are in it.

I have a dream that global warming stops,
That everyone is a friend,
Nobody steals and nobody kills,
I have a dream and they are in it.

I have a dream that everyone can be free,
Holidays are every day,
That insects don't scare,
I have a dream and everyone is in it.

What a perfect world it would be . . .
If all this happened in my dream.

Emma Jeffery (11)
Sandye Place School, Sandy

I Have A Dream

I have a dream that blossomed trees are everywhere,
I have a dream that the sun is up all day
And the moon is up all night,
I have a dream that a little 'Hey' was said by everyone
Every morning,
I have a dream that children can play alone safely outside,
I have a dream to be able to leave our bikes outside.
Without anyone stealing them,
I have a dream that there would be no arguments in the world,
I have a dream of no money problems in the world,
I have a dream of no terrorist attacks,
So people can feel safe,
I have a dream of no racist comments in the world,
I have a dream that everyone gets a change
To say a comment against something.
I have a dream that everyone has a peaceful, quiet life,
I have a dream that one day, just one day,
All of my dreams will come true.

Rioni Williams (11)
Sandye Place School, Sandy

My Dreams

I have a dream that everyone would have a full tummy like mine,
I have a dream that everyone would just talk to each other,
Instead of using violence,
I have a dream that everyone would have a house and a job,
I have a dream that everyone would not get or catch diseases,
I have a dream that everyone only made drugs that
Could help you get better, and not ones which can kill you.

My dreams are now over
And I hope that everyone
Has a nice life forever.

Jessica Brown (11)
Sandye Place School, Sandy

I Had A Dream

One day I had a dream . . .
That the world would be a better place,
No gangs,
No arguments for poverty,
No men to rape little children,
The worst, no bombing,
The streets have no rubbish scattered around,
All the homeless were no more
And everyone has what they need
And everyone was equal.

What needs to be better?
Our friendships,
Our environment
And clubs to keep children off the streets,
To stop gangs that kill
And everything's bad,
Then everything would be better . . .

Camellia Fage (11)
Sandye Place School, Sandy

I Have A Dream . . .

I have a dream that one day,
Smoking will be banned,
Bullying will be stopped,
No chewing gum on the floor,
No spitting in our environment
And no drinking underage,
No taking drugs when not needed,
Graffiti off the walls,
No litter on the floor and
No wars in Iraq.

Kelly Evans (11)
Sandye Place School, Sandy

I Have A Dream

I have a dream that children can play in their homes
Or street without fear,
I have a dream that if one man speaks out,
His voice would echo through a nation,
I have a dream that the homeless and starving world
Would become the homeowners and be well fed,
But then I wake up, and it's so bad I would
Choose to dream again . . .

I have a dream that the people who claim they
Are rich and famous would be treated as equals,
I have a dream that pollution and worries would
Become happiness and joy,
I have a dream that people from all over the world
Of all races could come together and unite,
But then I wake up, and it's so bad I would
Choose to dream again . . .

I have a dream that if one human is hurt,
People all over the world would aid him,
I have a dream that men and women of all ages,
Could sit and be equal,
I have a dream that when a man is grown,
He would respect those younger as he would himself,
But then I wake up, and it's so bad I would
Choose to dream again . . .

I have a dream that my friends and I could play without
Fear of anything,
I have a dream that if my message was heard by one person,
It would be heard by a nation,
I have a dream that if I were ever hungry or needy,
My hunger would be fed and my needs taken care of,
But then I wake up, and it's so bad I would
Choose to dream again . . .

Nigel Adams (12)
Sandye Place School, Sandy

I Have A Dream

I have a dream . . .
That the falling of bombs,
Is replaced by the falling of petals,
That all hate and war,
Turns to love and happiness,
Why does war exist?
We live in a world where races matter,
Why can't it just change?
Little things make war,
Well I say water the world,
Let things grow, but keep things orderly,
So nothing can start a war,
Ask yourself, are one or two people,
Worth over 15,000 people's lives?
Well I say, 'No, no, no!' Do you?
Well, you should,
Would you like to be split up from your family,
Never to see them again,
Just because you worship a religion?
Then someone kills you, it's unfair you might think,
You might not care now,
But when someone you love gets killed,
You will care, it would be the most important thing in the world,
Think of Anne Frank and the war,
She got locked up because she believed in something different
And because she was a Jew,
Religion, football, race, colour, food, is it really worth it?
Ask yourself that.
I'm not saying be robots, all the same,
Just don't argue, it might turn into a war some day,
That is my dream, so can you help me to make it happen today?
This will not wait, so get up and help today.

Lucy Barringer (13)
Sandye Place School, Sandy

I Have A Dream . . .

I have a dream to put things right,
Killings, war, terrorism, illness and I'm going to fight,
Bombing London and the railways,
Why can't they just stay away?
I dream of a world where none of this happens.

I have a dream where war won't start,
Why can't they just have a heart?
That nightmare, that we all fear,
If you think about it, it's getting near,
I dream of a world where none of this happens.

I have a dream where we have cures for all illnesses,
Of many people mending their ways,
People dying and suffering, every day,
Is this how it should be?
I dream of a world where none of this happens.

I have a dream where killings are not here,
See this is what we all fear,
Walking down the alleyways,
It could happen, one of these days,
I dream of a world where none of this happens.

I have a dream where racism is a thing of the past,
Where people don't have to run away fast,
Calling people names, it's just not right,
That is why we have got to fight,
I dream of a world where none of this happens.

I have a dream where none of this happens,
No racism, illness, war or killings or terrorism,
So this is where my message ends
And I'm going to say,
'Are you going to help me find a way?
And I want it to happen now and today?'

Natalie Broughall (13)
Sandye Place School, Sandy

I Have A Dream

I have a dream that no shops will get lifted,
That all kids could run and not get bullied,
So all listen to me now,
As I tell you about my dreams.

I have a dream that all diseases will go,
That no people will die,
So find the answer,
To stop this cancer.

I have a dream that all black people
And white people could play together,
So don't judge by the colour of other's skins,
Look deep down within.

I have a dream that any case of
Mugging is what's in a living room cabinet,
So don't hit someone because of what they are,
Be kind and compliment them.

I have a dream that anyone who is murdered,
Can come back and live their full life,
So put down your gun and
Put things behind you.

I have a dream that no one
Will be judged as a *minger*,
So don't say that nasty word,
Just be nice.

I have a dream that drugs,
Will all of a sudden just vanish,
So put down that cocaine
And go outside and live again.

So listen to what I have to say
And put it into action - *today!*

Jake Cooper (12)
Sandye Place School, Sandy

I Have A Dream

I had a dream that there was no hatred in the world
And everyone was equal, but then I woke up
And found it was only a dream.

I had a dream that there were no wars, killings, violence
And stealing, but then I woke up and found it was only a dream.

I had a dream that there was no racism or prejudice,
But then I woke up and found it was only a dream.

I had a dream that everyone agreed that there should
Be no deformation so all the wildlife would be safe,
But then I woke up and found it was only a dream.

I had a dream that the proud lion could still roar like
The real king of the jungle and poaching would stop,
But then I woke up and it was only a dream.

I had a dream that there was no weapons like the pistol
Which can certainly kill but then I woke up
And found it was only a dream.

I had a dream that there was no global warming,
But then I woke up and found it was only a dream.

I had a dream that there was no litter or pollution,
But then I woke up and found it was only a dream.

I had a dream that there was no poverty or poorness in Africa
But then I woke up and found it was only a dream.

I had a dream that there was no whale hunting
And instead we could do relaxing things in a pool
But then I woke up and found it was only a dream.

I had a dream that there was no illness at all,
Whether you are big or small
But then I woke up and found it was only a dream.

I had a dream that we could take everything back
But that was only a dream,
In that dream, I thought we could make it
And then I woke up and said,
'We can make it better!'

Jack Parish (11)
Sandye Place School, Sandy

I Have A Dream

I have a dream that one day war will stop and no one will get shot,
I have a dream that bombs will get thrown away,
That one day torture will not see another day,
I have a dream, knives will snap and guns will crack,
I have a dream that cruel teachers will cry
And horrible features will die,
I have a dream that I could fly and no one will die,
I have a dream that politics would stop and
Animals wouldn't get shot,
I have a dream that everyone could have money
And everything would be happy and funny,
I have a dream that no one could get an illness
And people who steal would confess,
I have a dream that they will show racism a red card
And for people to stop drugs - although it's very hard.

I have a dream . . .

Robert Tant (12)
Sandye Place School, Sandy

I Have A Dream

I used to have a dream,
It was to own a power station,
It would generate electricity,
Enough to power the nation.

Then one day it happened,
My dream faded away,
I learnt about global warming
And to stop it, we must pay.

I now have a dream,
To rescue the Earth
And return it to the state
It was at its birth.

Scott Parsons (13)
Sandye Place School, Sandy

Hope For The Future

The future looks dark,
Full of war, death and disasters,
Ruined, spoilt and killed by us,
Destroying our planet.

Our future looks black with pollution,
Houses and factories fill the places where
Forests and fields once were,
The wildlife gone forever.

But there's still hope . . .

It's up to us to save our future,
To fill it with light,
We can save our oceans,
We can save our trees,
We can still save our souls.

There's still hope . . .

The future could be bright for us,
Keep the fields and the forests
And get rid of the factories, death and war,
Have peace and happiness and love.

There's hope now . . .

Now the future looks brighter,
With the happiness in us,
With love in the air
And peace for all.

The future looks brighter and better now . . .

Jordan Harrington (11)
Sandye Place School, Sandy

I Have A Dream

I have a dream
That cancer would disappear,
But to do that we need to get the right gear,
I have another idea that would be great,
If it came true and that is to get rid of the flu,
More doctors is what we need,
To stop death and to plant a new life seed,
I have another dream,
That people would stop calling racist names,
It isn't laughter, fun and games,
It's for real,
Because people can feel
So just lock up the racist guys
And for punishment stuff their face full of pies,
Another idea,
Is to rid the world of fear,
We should stop terrorists,
We should teach them a lesson,
For messing,
I have another dream,
That we could stop war,
If we do, people will want power, no more,
To do that, give each country money,
For them, if it's raining, inside will still be sunny,
My last dream is,
To stop bullying and name-calling,
Then people's hopes will rise instead of falling
And they are my dreams,
That I always see,

Brett Slater (13)
Sandye Place School, Sandy

I Have A Dream . . .

I have a dream,
That the world is perfect,
But it isn't,
There's wars, terrorists and racism,
Bad words, bombs and litter,
No one could change it,
No one could live it,
So all they can do is die,
No one can live this way,
If you can, you're stupid.

There's homelessness and hunger,
Nastiness and stupidness
And that's so immature,
Don't sit back and watch TV,
You have to help the poor,
Fires, guns and burglars,
Armour, weapons and shields,
To help the bad people,
But what weapons do we have?
Basically just be good,
Just be kind
And don't go wild,
Because we have nature
And nature's beautiful.

Danielle Coveney (13)
Sandye Place School, Sandy

I Have A Dream . . .

I have a dream . . .
That there will be no hatred between each other
And that we all get along,
I have a dream . . .
That there will be no guns, wars or violence in the world,
I have a dream . . .
That there will be no more murders or racist comments in our world,
I have a dream . . .
That there will be no stealing in the world,
So everyone could be so trusted,
I have a dream . . .
That there would be no pollution in the world
And to stop the global warming.

That's my dream.

Jasmine Phillips (12)
Sandye Place School, Sandy

I Had A Dream

I had a dream that there would be no more violence in the world,
I had a dream that there would be no more abuse on children,
I had a dream that everyone would be happy for the rest of their lives,
I had a dream that I lived in Hollywood with all the celebrities,
I had a dream that everyone would sleep peacefully,
Under the beautiful stars,
I had a dream that I won a million pounds and gave it to
All the children that were in need.

Rosemary Robertson (12)
Sandye Place School, Sandy

I Have A Dream . . .

I have a dream of freedom,
Freedom far from the inevitable end.

I have a dream
That all the world cries together,
A symphony of sobbing
And where the evil have slashes down their sides,
That we may recognise them by their weeping.

I have a dream,
Of unicorns and rainbows,
Where there's no need to strip away the masks,
To find the real you.

I have a dream,
That people will wake up and smell the poison,
Realise what they've done is a crime.

I have a dream that we will live our lives,
Rather than criticising our friends.

I have a dream we break down the walls,
Because reinforcements don't arrive until you call them.

I have a dream,
That happiness is the only drug.

I have a dream that we will fight with words, wit and music,
The whole world is a contest, leave your brutality
Behind you and prove yourself.

I have a dream the finger of blame lies undecided,
It takes two to tango, you know.

I have a dream of honesty
So hold my hand and tell me you love me.

I have a dream which I will follow,
Though it's slippery and though it's shy,
I will be stepping on its heels,
Dreaming . . .
Dreaming . . .

Pippa Bransfield-Garth (13)
Sawston Village College, Sawston

I Have A Dream

I have a dream of chocolate,
Milky, sweet and smooth,
Where taste buds flourish and dance
And all are indulged in happiness.

I have a dream of freedom,
A life where no one is trapped,
A world where no one is hurt
And children laugh all day.

I have a dream of sleep,
Blissful silence,
Fabulous dreams
And a world where imagination rules.

I have a dream of love,
Where no one is challenged,
Where everyone is accepted
And justice is the word.

I have a dream of music,
Beautiful, calm, classical,
Heavy metal, rock
And sweet jazz 'n' blues, floating in the air.

I have a dream of trust,
Where lies do not exist,
Friendships so strong, nothing can break them
And be reunited as one.

Kirstie Bransfield-Garth (12)
Sawston Village College, Sawston

I Have A Dream

All I dream of is . . .

A chocolate river, rippling slowly through my garden,
A money tree with juicy fifty-pound notes,
A shopping centre, where you can buy everything, for nothing.

All I hope for is . . .

A world with no poverty or racism,
Where helpless animals are not rejected,
Where sins are forgiven and forgotten.

All I wish for is . . .

A beautiful Palomino pony, galloping on the golden beach,
A silent wave tickling my feet,
A diamond rainbow, stretching through the silver sky.

All we deserve is . . .

A world where we put an end to war and punishment,
Where no man dies because of our selfishness,
Where we live in peace
And where our dreams become reality.

Emily Driscoll (12)
Sawston Village College, Sawston

Look Both Ways

Look both ways, before you cross the road,
You don't want to get hit by a heavy load.

Look both ways, from head to toe,
Human weaknesses are starting to show.

Look both ways, to our world and theirs,
We eat, they starve, nobody cares.

Look both ways to the ground and the sky,
Factories pump, ozone rises, animals die.

Look both ways, from present to future,
We need to change, can we get there?

Tom Bell (13)
Sawston Village College, Sawston

Gone

Gone in a *sparkle*, a *splish* and *splash*,
Peace has trickled from our lands.

Gone in a *skip*, a *leap*, a *stroll*,
Love has dripped from our hearts.

Gone in a *flash*, a *bang*, a *swoop*,
Justice has flown away.

Gone in a *smack*, a *slap*, a *swish*,
Sanity has jumped out the window.

Gone in a *second*, a *minute*, an *hour*,
Loyalty has spun through the walls.

Gone from our hearts, from our souls,
From the world,
Dreams have vanished . . .

Ben Miller (13)
Sawston Village College, Sawston

Dreams That Flow

I have a dream,
Where ink flows thick,
In seas and rivers
And creativity is free,
To roam on plains,
Of paper white.

I have a dream,
Of spears tipped
With blue blood,
Creating a new world
Where quarrels of men and women
Are never to infect.

Zuhair Crossley (11)
Sawston Village College, Sawston

I Wish . . .

I wish I could . . .
Fly to the end of the universe,
Jump from a 90-foot building
And get up without a scratch,
Dive into a pool of sherbet.

I wish I could . . .
Walk off the world
And walk back on in 1000 years,
Build a golden palace out of fudge,
Climb Mount Everest in a single leap.

I wish I could . . .
Never grow old and stay a lively child forever,
Build a thriving city on the moon,
Drink pure sugar, straight from the cane.

I wish I could . . .
Live in a world that reigns,
Without terror,
Dream in a world, that had plentiful food,
Ride in a world where freedom rules.

Alix Schwiening (13)
Sawston Village College, Sawston

Don't Dream

I'm not going to dream,
Seems to me, the world's a mess,
Someone has to do something,
Before it's too late,
What is a dream?
Hiding from the world.

I'm not going to dream,
Global warming is real,
Melting the ice caps,
We must end pollution,
What is a dream?
Shunning responsibility.

I'm not going to dream,
Poverty all around,
War and death,
Everyone's problem,
What is a dream?
Walking away.

So I'm not going to dream,
I'm going to speak, help, work, feed, cure and act.

You. Me. Everyone. We can save the world.

David Ford (12)
Sawston Village College, Sawston

Incomplete

You have been told,
About Africa, India, Asia, Iraq,
But have you been told,
About the troubles of smack?
Imported from afar,
An eastern domain,
Across Iranian borders,
By those with no name.

So here it arrives,
After travelling afar,
Now a liquid substance,
Powdery so far,
Off to the user,
One squeeze is all it takes,
For some light relief,
But what are the stakes?

A visual absurdity,
A colourful blur,
Out into a coma,
Death yet to confer,
No one to notice,
Until stench runs the streets,
Until bodies are uncovered,
Families, now incomplete . . .

Spinoza Pitman (13)
Sawston Village College, Sawston

Sheep

Everyone is a sheep,
Governed by their farmers,
Afraid to be individual,
Adamant routines,
Following the flock,
Dumb to being used,
Lambs to the slaughter,
Profits for the rich,
No time for thought,
Lies spun to the young,
Growing up deaf to the truth,
No control over their lives,
Imprisoned by blind authority,
Why?
Why is everyone scared to make the move that sets them free?
Why is everyone scared to speak up and be heard?
Be individual,
Be heard,
Be seen,
Don't be a sheep!

Tom Champness (15)
Sawston Village College, Sawston

What Will Happen?

What will happen if racism thrives?
What will happen if love dies?
What will happen if war carries on?
What will happen when compassion's gone?

What will happen when generosity is abolished?
What will happen when the ozone layer's demolished?
What will happen when prejudice wins?
What will happen if patience is binned?

What will happen if the sea were to evaporate?
What will happen when the world is controlled by hate?
What will happen when fossil fuels run out?
What will happen if we have a worldwide drought?

What will happen to the starving in Africa?
What will happen to the rainforest massacre?
What will happen to the broken food chains?
What will happen to the innocent minds in pain?

The end of the world?
You decide . . .

Sam Fleck (13)
Sawston Village College, Sawston

Words To Change The World

Words to change the world,
That's what this poem's about,
But how is it possible to change,
A world so full of doubt?
And hate and also bloody war,
Honour and kindness exist no more,
So how can we begin to change,
The practice of the centuries?
How strange that politicians quibble and fight,
With no solution yet in sight,
But do not fear, each one of us,
Can help, in you, each one I trust,
To do right by our cause,
To right wrongs and uproot laws
And struggle till we see the light,
Of a pure world, not yet in sight,
A new beginning for one and all,
Creatures big and creatures small,
So maybe our beloved world,
Cannot be changed by only words.

Rhys James (13)
Sawston Village College, Sawston

Last Night I Had A Dream

Last night I had a dream . . .
Men fought men, over the colour of their skin,
Women and children lived in slums,
With no clean water or proper food,
Trees were cut down, just for the comfort of a fire,
Men blew themselves up just to make a point over religion,
The ice caps were melting, flooding coastlines and
Killing wildlife all because of,
Pollution, damaging the ozone layer, forever
Increasing the heat of the sun's rays,
Last night all I saw was violence and destruction,
Then I woke up and realised my dream was not a
Dream at all, but reality,
A nightmare!

Alex Scally (14)
Sawston Village College, Sawston

I Have A Dream

Last night while I was sleeping in my bed,
A dream came into my head,
The dream was strange,
The dream was funny,
I dreamt about a six foot orange bunny!

He had big teeth
And a big bushy tail,
He had small beady eyes
And a huge tongue the size of his two feet.

He stamped his feet and it moved the floor,
He hopped really high
And he yawned very loud
And he could lift heavy things that nearly touch
The sky.
The other rabbits were scared.

Sophie Banks (12)
Sawtry Community College, Sawtry

I Have A Dream

Last night I had an amazing dream,
So strange and unusual it did seem,
Something I had never thought before,
No shouting, no fighting and no war.

All was peaceful and all was calm,
No one now will come to harm,
No more pain for us to suffer,
We are all equals, no one tougher.

All the hatred, all the power,
Missiles shot into a shower,
Babies wailing, mother's crying,
Their fathers, husbands, out there dying.

This is the past and forgotten,
These memories will soon fade and be rotten,
Now every human in existence,
Will reach their life's potential distance.

Soldiers past, too late for some,
The smell of death no longer hums,
The world will be in constant peace,
A better place, to say the least.

We are all joined together in unity,
Blacks and whites in harmony,
Freedom of speech now causes no harm,
The world will forever be perfectly calm.

The world unites, they all join forces,
We have found the problem's source,
We all work together as a huge team,
That is my amazing, but halcyon dream.

Emma Ladlow (12)
Sawtry Community College, Sawtry

I Have A Dream

I have a dream,
I have it every night,
I'm walking down the street
And I suddenly take flight.

And suddenly I'm flying,
Drifting through the air,
Buildings like ants beneath me,
Wind whistling in my hair.

I watch the world from afar,
I watch the terror below,
People scream in fear,
As friend becomes foe.

People run from explosions,
People brandish knives,
What is the world coming to?
People taking other's lives.

And then the land changes,
Things get parched and dry,
Mothers trying to silence,
Their starving child's cry.

But then things change,
I lose all earthly sounds,
I slowly glide lower
And my feet touch the ground.

I am walking through the forest,
The grass rustles against my feet,
The trees tower way up high
And between them come pillars of light and heat.

I am surrounded by nature,
But there are humans too,
They look fresh and happy,
With possessions that aren't brand new.

They have no computer,
No plasma screen TV,
But the children are skipping,
Skipping with glee.

I sit down by a tree
And think what to do,
There's a world we've adapted to us
And one we're adapted to.

I decide to stay,
And take a wash in the lake that is our sink,
I sit on the bank
And I begin to think.

Now that I am here,
I can clearly see,
That people are only healthy,
When they are happy and free.

I awake

I have a dream.

Anelise Rosa (13)
Sawtry Community College, Sawtry

I Have A Dream

I have a dream . . .
To fly with the birds,
With their graceful and intriguing
Wings beating for what could be hours on end,
I have a dream . . .
To protect them from the evils of mankind,
To soar high above Man,
High above the clouds in the sky,
High above everyone and everything,
I'll do all in my power to protect and save bird kind,
Even if I die trying,
Because no one and nothing can stop me achieving
My dream!

Michael Gutsell (12)
Sawtry Community College, Sawtry

I Have A Dream . . .

I have a dream for me and you,
Holding hands, laying together,
Staying close, lips touched forever,
Your sweet smile in my mind,
Your soft hands all so kind,
The image of you in my head,
As we lay here on my bed,
Your lips resting on my wrist,
Flashbacks of our first kiss,
Shiny eyes staring at me,
Is this more than we're meant to be?
My dreams start to fade as I awake,
This reality is more than I can take.

Megan Curtis (13)
Sawtry Community College, Sawtry

I Have A Dream

I have a dream nearly every night,
That you're holding me so very tight,
We're stuck together just like glue,
Stuck that tight!

In my dreams you're keeping me warm,
On a long cold winter's night,
I know it's just a dream,
But hey it's mine!

It may be a dream,
It may be a fantasy,
But as long as I can see you,
I don't care what it is!

I have a dream . . .

Chelsea Owen (13)
Sawtry Community College, Sawtry

I Have A Dream

I have a dream where everyone's happy
And everyone has food and clean water,
But that dream is shattered, by people not helping
Others in the poorer countries of the world.

I have a dream where the air is very clean
And there's no litter on the floor,
But that dream is shattered when I open up the door
And people are driving cars and there's litter on the floors.

I have a dream where everyone's friends,
Doesn't matter what colour you are, or what your name is,
But that dream is shattered by people making fun of others,
Or using them as slaves because they're different.

I have a dream where children are all friends,
Doesn't matter if you're fat or thin,
But that dream is shattered by people making fun of others,
Just because they're different,
It doesn't give them the right.

I have a dream where there isn't any poverty,
Pollution, racism or bullying,
But that dream is shattered by people doing wrong,
Just because they think it's OK.

I have a question for those who do wrong,
'What have they ever done to you?'

I also have a message for those who are affected,
Hold your head up high and you can be proud for being
Like nobody else can.

Jordan Marsh (11)
Sawtry Community College, Sawtry

I Had A Dream

I had a dream last night,
That gave me quite a fright,
It was about a pixie which was very dipsy
And that was just one night.

It was very scary last night,
That dream which gave me a fright,
That poor little pixie, cannot be dipsy,
Perhaps she's not very bright.

As the dream I had last night,
Gave me a bit of a fright,
I won't dream it again tonight,
No way, I will stay awake till light.

Hannah Smith (12)
Sawtry Community College, Sawtry

I Have A Dream

I want to fly into the sky
And watch the world below go by,
Everyone scurrying around, like little ants,
Compared to being up here, down there is pants.

I want to lay on a cloud and have a kip,
The sun chasing away that chilly nip,
Chasing through the sky a shooting star,
I bet it could beat me though, by miles so far.

But to me it's a dream,
I'm afraid in all it seems,
As the only way to get there is by rocket,
But I don't think I'll get into the one
That's in my pocket.

Jordan Cooke (13)
Sawtry Community College, Sawtry

I Have A Dream

I have a dream to walk out on the track,
To be in front of thousands.

I have a dream to be there when the gun is shot,
To hear the ringing through my ears.

I have a dream to run off with the wind in my hair,
With the cries of happiness in my ears.

I have a dream to sprint down the last leg,
Hearing my name being chanted.

I have a dream to finish seconds in front,
To wear the flag around me.

I have a dream to stand on the podium,
To hear the National Anthem.

I have a dream to be given the gold,
To win in front of thousands.

I have a dream to be in the Olympics,
To run for my country.

Penelope Ford (12)
Sawtry Community College, Sawtry

I Had A Dream

I had a dream one night,
That brought an enormous fright,
Lion-sized snails,
With shiny tails,
That I fought off with all of my might.

I had a dream one afternoon,
These scary creatures were in my room,
My sword I swung,
With the force of a ton
And brought these strange things to their doom.

Jessica Halley (11)
Sawtry Community College, Sawtry

I Have A Dream

What happens in dreams?
Will I sit on a cloud?
Is walking or talking
Or jumping allowed?

Will I be on my own,
Or with my friends?
Does it go on forever,
Or eventually end?

What happens in dreams?
Will I play a harp's strings?
I can't play piano,
I can't even sing.

Will I know who I am?
Will I know what I'm called?
If I pinch myself hard,
Will I feel it at all?

Emily Wilson (11)
Sawtry Community College, Sawtry

I Have A Dream

I've flown through the air,
Amongst the white clouds.

I've swam the deepest ocean,
Amongst the coloured fish.

I've climbed the highest mountain,
Reaching the top.

All in my dream.

Ben Reed (13)
Sawtry Community College, Sawtry

I Have a Dream

I have a dream for the Earth to become a world of peace,
like God intended.
I dream for a world without wars and violence.
As time goes on, there is more and more violence in the media
and on the streets.
I dream for a world without this.

I dream for a world without racism or any other discrimination.
I hope that in the near future that people can preach about peace,
and then make it true without a person who doesn't agree with them,
hurting them, or even . . . killing them!

I have a dream . . . for the world.

Fern Cornwall
Sawtry Community College, Sawtry

I Have A Dream

I have a dream that the people of the world
Are filled with kindness and love,
It doesn't matter if we are black or white,
We are all the same as one another,
So put the dark past of racism behind you,
So everyone can get along in the world,
With peace and love,
Then we can dream of a better world.

Leon Stenhouse (17)
Sunnyside School (SLD), Biggleswade

I Have A Dream

I have a dream where smoking is gone
And if so, I have won,
I dream of a world at peace
And that includes the east,
I dream of a world where people come together
And are there for each other,
I dream that my neighbourhood
Is free from violence,
So people can see how friendly it is,
I dream of Planet Earth's fine world,
Which should stay there forever.

Rory Simpson (14)
Sunnyside School (SLD), Biggleswade

I Had A Dream

I had a dream of a better place in the world,
A world with clean air and clean cities,
Don't leave rubbish everywhere, chuck it in the bin
At once and give us a pure, clean world,
This planet has to be tidy, if not the trees will die
And the water gets filthy, including the animals on
Land and on sea,
They will die as well, so please tidy up this world *now!*

Rosie Chappell (17)
Sunnyside School (SLD), Biggleswade

I Have A Dream

I have a dream that we could all live in harmony,
That no wars are fought,
I have a dream that peace and justice reigns everywhere,
That peace and justice is taught.

Bells would ring every day, no hatred anywhere,
The world in a golden age,
Corruption would be a thing of the past, joined by sorrow,
Evil lost on the other page.

I have a dream that we could all live in harmony,
That no wars are fought,
I have a dream that peace and justice reigns everywhere,
That peace and justice is taught.

Religion, faith and belief would work together,
The world run by love,
Happiness would be king and peace would be his queen,
The Earth's symbol a dove.

I have a dream that we could all live in harmony,
That no wars are fought,
I have a dream that peace and justice reigns everywhere,
That peace and justice is taught.

Hate would be replaced with love,
War replaced with peace,
Cruelty would be replaced with kindness,
Sorrow and corruption will cease.

I have a dream that we could all live in harmony,
That no wars are fought,
I have a dream that peace and justice reigns everywhere,
That peace and justice is taught.

As evil and hate walk hand in hand away,
Good and love walk hand in hand near,
Shadows of the world are vanquished and disappear,
Now no one has a need to fear.

James Barker (14)
Swavesy Village College, Swavesy